Yogesh Pearlal

SALES
SUPERSTAR

The Winning Formula to
Call Center Sales Success

red**Oystor**

London | Johannesburg | New York

Published by RedOystor Books
an imprint of RedOystor Media (Pty) Ltd

visit www.redoystor.com for more information
Or contact us at **www.redoystor.com/contact-us**

www.redoystor.com/SalesSuperstar
www.facebook.com/SalesSuperstar

Cover Design & Layout by
RedOystor Media (Pty) Ltd

Printed by **novus print**, a Novus Holdings company

Available on Kindle and other retail outlets

ISBN: 978-0-620-76546-6 (Print)
978-0-620-69701-9 (ePub)

Contents

You can be a 'star' or you can be a 'SUPERSTAR, the choice is still yours to make.

SALES SUPERSTAR

PREFACE

If there is anything I know better than any other thing, it is sales; more specifically over-the-phone sales in the call center.

Not to blow my own horn or anything, but for the many years that I have worked in a call center, on the phone armed with an ear piece and an arsenal of skills and techniques, I have sold anything and everything that can be sold over the phone, from cell phone contracts to car insurance and most recently life insurance.

I have to admit, my skills have improved over the years to the point where I can confidently say that I am probably one of the very few people who consistently make more money selling over the phone in a call center environment than any other high paying jobs that require very minimum educational qualifications as a point of entry.

Being able to make more money in the call center than most lawyers, doctors or even accountants, I have learned that with sales, particularly call center sales, success is not an event but the great reward of consistent performance over and over again.

I've been asked this question on many occasions, "HOW?" How do you keep doing the same thing over and over again and getting an even better result?

I believe, for the most part, people ask me this question because they want to know my secret to successful call center sales.

In this book, I will detail my response in the most simple manner, even as you read through page by page, you'll be amazed at how much common sense could simply just be that, COMMON SENSE!

Truth be told, this is in contrast to what we have been told or have been made to believe about call center sales, that it should be difficult, heartless or just pretty much a drag.

Today, even as I write this book, I can attribute my success in call center sales to what I have come to call the 'SALES SUPERSTAR WINNING FORMULA'.

Think of it in this way.

Think of the many movie greats, the likes of Chuck Norris, Sylvester Stallone (or Rambo as we all got to know him as kids) or that other guy with very fast moves, making martial arts look like a piece of cake, oh yeah him, that one, I know you can picture him, yes him Bruce Lee; or Jacky Chan for that matter.

All of them have something about them that makes them amazing SUPERSTARS. Their personality fits into their role so much so that even when scripted, their acting seems so natural.

The 'SALES SUPERSTAR WINNING FORMULA' comes from exactly that, it is about turning more sales calls into financial success by using your PERSONAL-ITY and SKILLS to move the sales process forward. Simply put, I've found that using your PERSONALITY to compliment your SKILLS is a very straight to the point approach to sales success.

I've made that FORMULA work for me by fine tuning my PERSONALITY and developing my SKILLS, and "Walla" I've made more money on the phone than many professionals can dream of. Not to insult your intelligence in any way, the pages that follow, I will share with you in detail how the "SALES SUPERSTAR WINNING FORMULA" has made me a successful sales person in the call center.

I know the word "FORMULA" creates the idea that this is some complicated mix of addition, subtraction or multiplication and division of some sort, designed to confuse your prospects into buying whatever it is you're selling. Much as I would like that to be true, I'm really not that much of a genius; but I do think that finding a way to successfully produce consistent results for making sales over the phone, now that is GENIUS.

The 5 Basic Principles of Success

Many sales gurus will tell you 'SALES' is just sales and that it doesn't matter what you are selling, how you are selling and to whom you are selling. I have a different view. Some sales people do better than others not because of their tactics but because of a combination of their SKILLS and PERSONALITY.

This is what makes them great salespeople.

If you're to become a Call Center SALES SUPERSTAR , you need to understand that you're going to have to work on a few basic principles. To get you started, focus on the following principles that I believe set all successful sales people apart from the not-so-successful sales people.

1. Decide that you will not let your past determine your future,
2. Decide on what you want and what kind of future you want and act on it,
3. Learn from the best and only the best, learn from people that are where you want to be,
4. Work hard to put what you have learnt into action to achieve your desired future, do what others won't so you can have what other don't
5. Do one thing every day that will get you closer to the future you want.

Happy selling.

After all, you were born to be a SUPERSTAR!

***

BELIEVING

is seeing the

IMPOSSIBLE

to be

POSSIBLE

INTRODUCTION

I have not always been the best sales person in the call center. In fact, when I started off I made many of the same mistakes I've seen new call center sales recruits make year after year.

Let's be honest, working in the call center is not exactly every child's dream, it was never mine but after discovering that I could make as much money as any other profession selling over the phone, I decided this is what I wanted to be good at.

I've gone beyond and made a great success of it. Today, I am writing a book about how you too can make call center sales the best experience.

The Oldest Profession

Sales and prostitution may very well be the oldest professions since the beginning of time, but neither of them is glorified positions, no pun intended.

Ask any call center agent why they chose to work in the call center, many of them will not easily admit, but the truth is, people who work in call centers think they are there not by desire but by circumstance.

Most call center sales agents have some story about why they work in the call center.

Their story will be anything and everything from "I am here to gain experience while I am studying to get a better job." Or "There was no other place I could get a job with my limited qualifications" or something along these lines.

Let's face it, every job situation has a story and call center sales is no different. Whatever your story, remember the 5 principles I mentioned in the pages before.

These principles will guide you towards finding your desired results.

1. Decide that you will not let your past determine your future,

2. Decide on what you want and what kind of future you want and act on it,

3. Learn from the best and only from the best, learn from people that are where you want to be,

4. Work hard to put what you learn into action to achieve your desired future, do what others won't so you can have what other don't

5. Do one thing every day that will get you closer to the future you want.

***

SALES SUPERSTAR

Chapter 1

DRIVING YOUR SUCCESS?

Before I can tell you how you too can become a call center SALES SUPERSTAR, let me tell you how I found myself in the place where I discovered my star qualities.

Growing up, I never really had much. There were days when we went without food or lights; somehow we made it because of sacrifices my mother made for her children to live to see another day. Going to bed with just a slice of bread and a cup of tea, I made a choice to change things around.

I became aware of what other people had, the good life, the fancy cars and all the money they wanted, I realized that just as much as I might not have the right background or work in a call center not by desire but by circumstance, I still had a CHOICE to make. I could not let my circumstances define who I was and who I wanted to be.

I had to make my 'circumstances' work for me. With that CHOICE I fell in love with working in the call center, and I have never looked back since.

The vibe, the buzz, the people; I fell in love with the idea that I could be of service to people who would be anywhere in the world. The challenge to become better than my past drove me to learn about how to better my SKILLS.

The desire to succeed made me harness my personality to get better at selling in the call center. Better than I had done before. My passion poured out with every word I spoke. With every sale I closed, my life changed one day at a time, or more like one SALE at a TIME. Here's how I changed my fate.

With the 5 principles I mentioned earlier, I made a CHOICE that my past will not determine my future, I made a DECISION on the future I wanted and to achieve that future I learnt from the best and only from the best, working very hard to do that one extra thing every day to get me to where I truly wanted to be.

All I needed was a reason to succeed, and that reason was my desire to have a better life for myself and for my family.

It begins with 'Why?'

The question you should wake up with very morning when you open up your eyes to a new day, ask yourself "why?"

'Why do you do what you do?'

'Why do you wake up day after day to report to your cubicle.'

You might think your answer is as simple as, 'To make money?' If MONEY is what you're looking for, ask yourself "Why do you want that MONEY?"

What is it that money can do for you that you desire to have it by working in a Call Center.

REMEMBER! Money is the result of what you do, not why you do what you do. Understanding the purpose of your existence is the key to achieving a lot more success.

You can have whatever you WANT, by knowing WHY you want whatever it is that you say you WANT.

***

BELIEVE you can, and you're half way there

- Theodore Roosevelt

(26th President of the United States)

SALES SUPERSTAR

Chapter 2:

SALES ESSENTIALS

Being in sales does not come with the same prestigious title like being a Doctor, an Accountant or Banking professional. However, no business or company would survive without the function of sales people.

The perception that CALL CENTER SALES is a job for under-qualified or unqualified people does not hold well with me.

Many call center sales people might not have the highest qualifications in terms of college or university qualifications but the position of call center sales still requires an enormous amount of knowledge coupled with guts, persistence, vigor and tenacity to perform at your best.

It takes a really strong person to take one rejection after another and still continue to wake up every day to make another call knowing very well they face a full day of rejection.

What Selling is Really About

If you've been in any position where you were either selling something or were in the process of being SOLD something, you'd agree that what you're selling matters just as much as WHO is selling.

SELLING IS ABOUT communicating the right messages to your buyer, connecting your product or services to their need to satisfy a particular desire.

SELLING IS ABOUT influencing buying decisions and persuading people to cooperate with you to do the things you want them to do.

SELLING IS ABOUT finding a need and meeting the desired expectation with the best possible solution to your buyer's needs and wants.

SELLING IS ABOUT convincing people that what you're selling will benefit them either by reducing pain or increase pleasure.

With Call Center Sales, the combination of PERSONALITY and SKILLS proves to be a winning formula to closing more sales than the average call center sales agent.

Call Center Sales Essentials

While doing some research on what really makes a person working in a call center more successful where others have failed?

Apart from the many skills and tactics you will learn with the 'SALES SUPERSTAR WINNING FORMULA' I've found that PERSONALITY plays a very big role. People are different, while I'll be the first to accept that, much as I have made a great success with my PERSON-ALITY, other personalities are just as successful. Personality is not something that can be taught, but surely there are ways in which it can be molded to suit the needs of your call center sales career.

This book is not about PERSONALITY but skills that compliment your personality. In order to achieve Call Center sales success, I will share with you personality traits that make a successful call center SALES SUPER-STAR.

The Power of PERSONALITY

I find a useful comparison in successful call center selling to that of baking. I am not the best in the kitchen but I've learned a thing or two about mixing recipes to get the desired result.

Not all bakers are the same, their personalities are different and given the same recipe each one would deliver the same kind of bake with a twist depending on their PERSONALITY. Anyone who's seen the TV show 'The Great British Baking Show' will tell you how the different competing bakers are given the same recipe but the results differ because of the baker's PERSONALITY.

If you're already working in the call center and want to increase your success in call center sales, or if you're thinking of joining a call center sales team, then knowing what is ESSENTIAL to your success will make your work or transition easy.

Know what is needed to succeed. Apply what is essential and you will succeed. These are the four ES-SENTIALS to your success in working in the call center environment:

Motivation - Know WHY you're selling

Competence - Know WHAT you're selling

Personality - Know WHO you're selling

External Factors - Know WHERE you're selling

Let's get you started with the MOTIVE for why you want to be successful in sales.

Motivation - Know WHY you're selling

I stand to be corrected, but was it Albert Einstein that said: "doing the same thing over and over again and expecting a different result amounts to insanity." Not exactly the same words but to paraphrase his thoughts I understand why he had that crazy look.

MOTIVATION speaks to your motive to succeed and how that fits with your job specifications and requirements, cultural fit as well as how your personal interest are best served by what you do.

Working in a call center sales environment is not suited to everyone but that doesn't mean the job cannot be done by anyone.

Understanding what MOTIVATES you is essential to your success. Understand the following motivational fits will make or break your desire to work and succeed in a call center sales environment:

Job fit. Does your job motivate you to be the best you can be? Does it challenge you to get better each day? Is the nature of the work fueling your drive to succeed taking into account the constant monitoring, demands for promptness, endless pressure to perform, confinements to space, etc?

Environmental Fit. Settings such as seating arrangements, lighting, and general noise levels will play a huge role in how you keep motivated to work and succeed in the call center. If this does not fit what you expect of your working environment; chances are, you'll find it frustrating to be working in such an environment; and being frustrated will definitely limit your success.

Culture fit. When it comes to company culture, it can be difficult to find a perfect fit, mainly because the people you will work with come from different backgrounds and relate to each other differently.

Essential to your success in the call center is understanding how the culture of the company and the call center environment matches your individual priorities and interests? This includes the type of people who work there, how the call center management leads, company values and company commitment to employee development and training.

You may not always be able to choose who you work with or the type of people on your team but you can still decide and choose how you interact with each one of them in a way that will inspire and motivate your success.

Competence - Know WHAT you're selling

I'm sure you understand why competence is key to your success. COMPETENCE of what you're selling has the greatest impact on your overall performance. It forms the foundation of your success.

It is an indication of whether you have the skills, the knowledge and the ability required to deliver what is expected of you in the function of a call center sales agent. This includes technical knowledge of the product or services your company offers, as well as knowledge of various call center systems such as computers, telephony systems, and customer relationship management (CRM) databases; all of which can easily be taught and tested for.

COMPETENCIES also reflects your ability to speak clearly and articulate your sales message with a passion that meets and exceeds your customer's expectations, along with the ability to develop a much-needed connection with every caller.

It involves solving problems and managing difficult situations to end every call in a positive manner; turning complaints into compliments and driving additional sales. Finally, but not least of all, COMPETENCE involves being able to multi task, often navigating multiple software applications while on the phone with your client. COMPETENCE cannot be achieved through reading of books and studying company product materials. It comes with practice and experience.

In order to increase my success working in the call center, I made it a point to understand the industry, how it works and how it relates to other industries.

To give you an understanding of what I mean, my current position as a Life Insurance Call Center sales advisor, my KNOWLEDGE of HOW Life Insurance works is such that when a client nominates an underage child as a beneficiary, I make a point to mention the need for a Will to inform Estate Executors how the funds should be used for beneficiaries under the age of majority.

Most people would think I have no business talking

about Wills when selling Life Insurance, but having added knowledge gives my client confidence and comfort of knowing I am an expert in my field; which builds trust and loyalty.

The more competent you are about your product, the more competent you are with the needs of your customers and the benefits of your products and your industry at large, the more trust and loyalty you will receive from your clients.

The only reward I know to come from trusting and loyal customers are sales and more sales.

Personality - Know WHO you're selling

I've touched a little on personality earlier and will go a little bit more in detail when we unpack the SALES SUPERSTAR SUCCESS FORMULA.

Going back to the analogy of a Baker and his personality, in the call center sales environment Personality adds flavor to what you're selling. It brings to life the message of influence on what you want your prospects to buy.

More than that, your personality affects your fitness to apply the knowledge of your product and its benefits, applying the sales process to deliver a message of influence on what you are selling.

Personality unlocks your potential where your skills are lacking when knowledge is still being acquired.

Even though one personality type may be more successful than another in a call center, whatever your personality, use what you have to make a success out of every call you make.

External factors

Some people may think external factors have no influence on work performance. Whatever your thoughts are on this matter, having worked in many different call centers, I've come to realize that if traveling to work and back is an issue of being stuck in endless traffic or unreliable public transport; chances are, you'll be frustrated by the thought of going to work.

I mention this because one of the decisions that led to more success in my career was moving closer to work so that I did not have to travel long distances to get to work. This might not be possible for everyone but it is worth mentioning that external factors may influence your success.

Learning to deal with the different external factors will improve your success in more ways than you can think. Where you can change the factors that influence your working performance, change them, where you cannot, learn to live with them by finding ways to work around them.

Many solutions are available for transport and many of the other external factors that influence your work performance. So, if public transport is an issue, see if you can't join a lift club. If living close to work is something worth considering, maybe share a place with a working buddy during the week and weekends you're back home.

Whatever the case may be, there is always a solution to working around External Factors that influence your working performance.

***

"The key to success is to focus our conscious mind on the things we desire not on the things we fear"

- Brain Tracy

What makes a Sales Superstar?

Chapter 3:

THE ART OF SELLING

I read somewhere that "even though people hate being sold to, they love to buy". More puzzling is the idea that we've become so consumed by technology recent studies show that a person picks up their phone an average of 86 times on any given day.

We wait on our phones to ring at any given time ready to hear great stories about how someone might have posted something interesting on their social media profile.

We eagerly wait to see if that one person we have been waiting to call the entire day bothered to send a message, be it text or instant messaging.

We browse on our cell phones for items that we might be interested in buying.

At one point the Blackberry phone was known to induce the 'Red Light Syndrome' - where Blackberry users were so consumed by the desire to see that RED LIGHT as an indication a message had just come in.

Our appetite to hear someone present us with something of interest has created such eagerness in our everyday interaction with our phones - more especially our mobile phone. When that call does finally come and the person on the other side of the line says something like "Good morning Mrs. Jones, my name is John Doe from the ABC Company ..." suddenly the "I AM NOT INTERESTED" wall goes up.

As a sales person, especially one who sells over the phone and mainly over the phone, your job is to overcome this great wall of "I AM NOT INTERESTED" by being the best, the biggest and the most awesome PERSONALITY there can be.

Your job is not just to be the star of your product or service but to be the "SUPERSTAR" to your client's needs, desires, and WANTS.

Do or die

A couple of years ago, a study was done by a prestigious American university about the main reasons why 9 out of 10 businesses fail within the first five years of operations. With all the resources any starting business can require, from funding to printers, computers, telephones, offices space and a lot more, still 9 out of 10 times the business will not survive to see more than 5 years.

Here's why, because the business had no sales.

With no sales, no business can start, grow, strive or even survive because sales are the lifeblood of any business.

You're the Life Blood of the Company

It's funny that many people who apply for the position of Call Center SALES in many instances never really understand the main function of their roles.

After all, there is a reason why you would be called a "SALES" person; because your main function is to make sales. Without selling, you will not survive to see another month. If anyone can remember the movie starring Will Smith, "Pursuit of Happiness"; if I remember correctly, there is a scene where his character walks door to door selling medical equipment which he had to sell just to survive. On the day he did not make a sale, he had to find accommodation in a public toilet for himself and his son.

This scene defines the importance of sales, and in the call center, you need to make the sales, or soon you will find yourself accommodated in the 'RESTROOM' of some public toilet.

DO make that call or your business of earning an income will die.

Do make the effort to close at least 3 times before you can call it a follow-up.

DO follow up with that client that said to call later or your source of income will die.

DO make an effort to learn how to connect with your client or your sales will not survive.

Unless you are making sales, the company you work for may soon fail and your source of income will die.

There's a very good reason why you're called a SALES PERSON and not a TELL person. You're paid to SELL not paid to TELL.

So 'Less Telling, MORE SELLING.' or more like "STOP TELLING, START SELLING."

Sales people do more selling as they are talking and for that reason to be a sales SUPERSTAR, you'll need to make the phone your stage, the place where you transform and become the solution to your client's needs and want.

***

Chapter 4

WHERE SALES COME FROM

I'm very optimistic about the prospects of every call being a sale, and I say this with the greatest amount of respect for the reality on the sales call.

I read this in a book on cold calling sales techniques by Stephan Schiffman about the different types of sales. Even as I borrow some of his knowledge I have tried my best to simplify this for easy understanding for the call center sales environment.

There are 3 types of sales available to any sales person who operates in the call center sales environment, and they are:

1. The Sale You Want,
2. The Sale You Can't Get and,
3. The Sale You Must Get.

Still don't get it, don't you worry, I will explain.

Before I can do that, allow me enlighten you to a new age of buying and selling in a world filled with technology and highly connected consumers.

What You Should be Selling

In this day and age, people don't buy what they NEED, they buy what they WANT. The old way of selling on NEEDS is almost dead. Knowing how to understand what your client WANTS is what will set you apart from your peers.

Truth is, people need to eat more healthy food but that doesn't mean they will. It's what they NEED but not necessarily what they WANT.

The same applies to any product sold in a call center. People need car insurance, but do they want it, not necessarily. People need life insurance but do they WANT it, not entirely.

Understanding what a client WANTS and what a client NEEDS will set the bar for how you make your sales.

You have 3 sales at your disposal. Each one has its challenges and its lessons. Close 1 of the 3, you are only as good as any other call center sales person – you're a STAR.

Close 2 of the 3 sales available to you; suddenly you become the SALES SUPERSTAR.

The last of the 3, don't worry too much about that one, it was never meant to be yours in the first place. But if you do close that one too, count your lucky stars and make a run for the wind.

1. The Sale You Want

This sale is the kind of sale that even as you connect with your prospect on the other side of the line, you are exactly what the client has been looking for and has been WANTING; and you just happened to be at the right place at the right time.

Put simply, for any product or service, whatever the product or service might be, there is a buyer ready and willing to buy and all you have to do is, be there at the right place and time.

Think of this sale as the low hanging fruit.

To prove my point – stand on the side of the road with a cup in hand where people are walking by, chances are there will be someone who will put some money in your cup without you ever saying a word.

This is the sale you want and enjoy. Not much work is needed on your side.

To my experience and with the expectation that every call will turn into a sale, I look forward to this sale because it is the confirmation that my product or service has a market.

2. The Sale You Can't Get

This sale I enjoy the least but look forward to on a day to day basis. "Why?" you might ask.

One reason and one reason alone, it is the kind of sale that humbles me with a reminder that life is not perfect, and neither is 'Sales'. Often, with this kind of sale, I would say to my client, "Even if I gave you this product for FREE, you still wouldn't take it."

And the prospect would confirm with a resounding "YES". After all, it's not what they NEED or WANT.

The is no real connection to providing a solution to their problem.

3.   The Sale You Must Get

Every sale is worth fighting for, and every sale deserves the same amount of energy and expectation that "This is the one."

The MUST GET sale is what makes stars into "SUPERSTARS". Allow me to explain why.

The best call center sales people I know are able to identify what a client WANTS and align that to a NEED and also connecting that to a solution on offer in the first few seconds of the call.

With the sale that never was, the WANT and the solution are incompatible, with the SALE that MUST be, the NEED is there, it is only a question of "Does the client WANT your solution?"

The sale 'you must get' makes you a SALES SUPERSTAR because you have thoroughly assessed what your client WANTS, aligned that to a specific NEED and you found your solution to be highly compatible; however your client is not able to see the compatibility.

Let's face it, if you can turn that "would be sale" into a SALE, you would do better than most call center sales people if you simply learn how to create compatibility for what your client WANTS and the solution you offer.

"SUPERSTAR" performance comes with you being able to turn the "MUST GET" sale into a SALE because with 2 out of 3 sales, you are guaranteed to out-perform the average call center sales person. This is where the SALES SUPERSTAR WINNING FORMULA comes into play.

Identifying What Your Customer WANTS

If you ask any client on the phone what it is they really WANT chances are you'll be flooded with a multitude of responses. You might be left wondering whether or not you can truly satisfy those WANTS.

When it comes to NEEDS I think we can all agree that over the years we've kind of come to an agreement on what the client NEEDS. But with the change in customer awareness and behavior, you'd consider that it's time we look beyond what the client NEEDS with a focus on what the client WANTS.

So how do you know what your client WANTS?

A sure fire way of discovering what your client WANTS is by questions that are relevant to your solution. Ask relevant questions and you will discover what your clients NEED.

Probe a little more and you're bound to find out what they really WANT. Experience has taught me that figuring out what a client WANTS is not much of big deal.

To get the right compatibility, your OFFER must meet a minimum of 2 out of three of what your client WANTS. This is what your clients WANT:

a) Your Clients WANT something they value or can value

You've asked the question about your client's family structure "Are you married, do you have kids?" and they answered "YES." So you know they NEED life insurance.

What's going to get your client to say YES to your offer will be determined by what they VALUE about their family that will make them WANT to buy life insurance.

I've had one or two clients where regardless of what I say about them needing Life Insurance cover they just don't budge. But the minute I say, I will give you all your premiums back if you remain claim free for a number of years through our cash back option, suddenly they want in.

They NEED life insurance but they VALUED the cash back option more. See where I am going with this.

Clients VALUE their TIME so the speed of delivery is everything. They VALUE their freedom to move and be anywhere they want to be when they chose to be, so a replacement car option on their car insurance may very well be the VALUE they WANT.

Your clients VALUE the APPROVAL of their peers when it comes to buying luxury cars, fancy watches, new cell phone technology and a lot more. Clients VALUE a lot of things, but the underlying similarity is that they want something they VALUE or can VALUE.

b) Your Clients WANT something they can relate with or relate to.

A young person who's recently started working and has never had the experience of paying a medical practitioner out of their pocket may not RELATE to the need for medical aid insurance. However the young couple with two kids who fall ill every change of season will definitely RELATE.

When you say to the young employee, who hardly ever gets sick, "Can you imagine on a day you don't feel like going to work for whatever reason.

You know your manager needs a medical sick note if you don't show up, you can see the doctor without paying out of your pocket", not the best example, but surely this is something the young employee can RE-LATE to.

Clients RELATE to many things. Those that have lost a loved one who supported them financially can RE-LATE to the need for life insurance. Any client that has lost something of VALUE to theft, an accident or natural disaster will RELATE to the NEED for home contents or car insurance.

Ask questions that will help you understand what the client RELATES to and offer a solution that will solve a NEED your client can RELATE to.

c) Your Client WANTS something to make them feel good about themselves

Lastly, studies have shown that people buy for one of two reasons, to increase pleasure or to reduce pain. WANTING to feel good about themselves is one of the reasons why your clients will say YES to your offer.

I feel good about buying a new car, if that GOOD FEELING comes with taking out car insurance, I'll take it. I feel good about talking to my friends and sharing all kinds of stories about my life, if that GOOD FEELING comes with taking the unlimited data package with the new iPhone, I'll take it.

Part of the SALES SUPERSTAR WINNING FORMULA is about knowing what your product is. My product as you will learn is 'HAPPINESS' for a specific reason. I know that my clients like to feel good about what they buy, and if that comes with 'HAPPINESS', I'm sure they'll take it.

Time is Money

There's truth to the fact that in the call center sales environment, TIME IS MONEY. The less time you spend getting to the point of agreement where your client gives banking details and you confirm acceptance of your OFFER, the better.

Depending on what you're selling and how much detail is required to complete the sale, anything more than 35 minutes is too much to bear for the person on the other side of the phone.

The only reason you should be giving additional information outside of your script is if the client asks for such information.

Even then, K.I.S.S your client, KEEP IT SHORT and SIMPLE. Think back when you were buying bread for the first time, did you really need to know what ingredients went into the baking the bread, the processes that go into packaging it and getting it into the store.

Not really. But you bought the bread anyway. The same applies to buying a car, a house, a phone, insurance or the service to deliver the newspaper to your door.

You'll get the occasional client asking you to send them additional information about your product or service.

Your job is to read between the lines.

More often than not, what your client is telling you is that you have not been able to connect their NEED to your solution, and therefore the client does not feel they WANT your solution.

Maybe you've given too much information, they are confused about what it is that they're really buying.

Think of it this way, you call a client, you want to SELL them car insurance, all they want to know is that you will pay for the repairs to their car should they be involved in an accident, or provide a replacement option should their car be stolen or if and when some natural disaster strikes you will be there to compensate them for their loss.

Over and above that, all they want to know is how much it will cost.

Since TIME IS MONEY, keep track of how much time you spend selling yourself, selling your product and selling your company, and getting the clients commitment. As quickly as possible move the sales process along to commitment.

***

Success is a numbers game. The number of times you take a shot.

Chapter 5

THE NUMBERS GAME

When I started in the call center, I was coming from a retail environment where I was paid by the hour - minimum wage. I was happy to get a salary at the end of the month. I didn't worry much about results because all I had to do was show up and be counted. Whether or not I did more than I was supposed to, I still got paid the same rate as everyone else.

The only reason I looked forward to another day at work was the promise of a promotion and a better job and even then as I worked in a minimum wage job, I still put my best foot forward.

Working in Call Center SALES, my hard work started to pay off. The more I did, the more I got paid. With this, I learned to understand the numbers game of sales success.

LEAD SOURCES

The call center environment has two sources of leads, or potential buyers - inbound leads and outbound leads.

The difference between the two being, with inbound, the client calls you because they heard or saw somewhere that you may be able to provide a solution to their need or problem. With outbound, you generate the lead either through a cold calling process or calling existing clients to offer them additional solutions.

An example of the latter is where you call people from the yellow pages or if you have an existing database of clients i.e. selling life insurance to your existing car insurance clients. Simple to understand, right? Perfect.

Whatever your source of leads, you need to be aware of how the NUMBERS influence your success. For instance, it makes little or no sense to focus on doing quotes when in fact you get paid to make sales and not just quotes.

Even though every sale begins with a quote or estimate process, if you're a sales agent, SELLING is what you need to focus on. It also makes no sense to wait for calls if you're working in an outbound skill-set because you make sales by actually calling the prospect. Get the picture? I hope you do.

Numbers don't lie

Knowing what you know about numbers and how they affect your quest for CALL CENTER SALES SUCCESS, it's simple to understand that numbers 'DO NOT LIE'. "If you don't make the call, you can't expect to make any sales."

Likewise in an inbound skill-set, if you don't take any calls, don't expect to make any sales either.

I have a simple formula for any person wishing to be successful SELLING in the call center, and this formula is more important than anything you can think of:

L=C=P=S.

Put simply:

Leads = Calls = Prospects = Sales.

Without leads, you can't expect to make calls, without calling your leads, you can't expect to have prospects and without SELLING to your prospects, you can't expect to make any sales.

The simplest part of this formula is the L=C part.

If you want to be successful with CALL CENTER SALES, you need to call all your leads, regardless of how you feel about them or what previous experience has taught you about whatever lead you have at your disposal.

Let me explain why I say that.

In my first job working in the call center, our leads were nothing more than a piece of paper with telephone numbers on it. There was no name, address or anything that would leave room for bias on the sales agent's part. I made it a point (and still do) to call every lead for an opportunity to sell my service or product.

Later on, I moved to a company where we got names, surnames as well as ID numbers. I found that some of the SALES agents I worked with selected who to call. E.g with car insurance, the older you get, the more likely your insurance premium would be cheaper, so many of the other agents would prefer to call older prospects because they knew the sale might be easier than with a young person.

As I was coming from a call center where leads were nothing more than a telephone number to call , I never used any preconceived bias to call my leads. I called every and any lead I got and that made all the difference.

The second part of the formula, P=S;

With every call you make, chances are, not every person you call will answer the phone. Whenever you do get through to the prospect, your job is to turn that into a sale.

This is not to say that every prospect will buy, but the more prospects you speak to, the more you can sell, the better chances they will buy.

The more successful you will become.

Know your numbers

Do you know how many prospects you need to speak to, to get a sale? Do you know how many leads you need to call for an opportunity to SELL? If you don't, it's difficult to plan your working approach. Plus how would you know if your sales plan is working?

Depending on which skill set you're working, the numbers may vary.

For example, if you are working in an outbound skill set, dealing with cold leads only, chance are you would need to make a lot more calls to get to the prospect for an opportunity to make a SALE.

In my first job in the call center, at the beginning of each day you got an A4 paper with numbers on it. Your job was to call every number on that list. Whenever you were not able to get hold of the lead, you wrote a note to try again later. With every list that had 50 numbers to call, on average I was able to speak to 30 prospects and make 5 sales a day.

So my SALES NUMBERS looked something like this; 50 leads, 30 prospects and 5 sales - a ratio of 50:30:5. By the end of the week, my numbers looked something like this 250:150:25. Every day was not the same, but I stuck to my numbers. Soon I learned to measure myself.

On those days when I made 5 sales before completing my list of 50 calls, I still made sure I make 50 calls for that day to meet my calling quota. If you woke me up in the middle of the night, I'd be able to tell you what my success number is - 50:30:5.

By the end of the week, if I had not made 25 sales, I made the extra effort to get my numbers right, meeting the minimum and never achieving less than what my numbers required.

Why is it important to stick to your numbers?

Suppose I didn't make those 50 calls, would I be able to reach my 30 prospects, maybe yes, maybe no, but then the following day my standard would have been lowered.

Success is not the result of a successful event but the habits that lead to that successful event. Make a habit of meeting your calling quota, your prospect quota and sales quota and you will be amazed at how successful you'll become.

Knowing your numbers is not supposed to keep you on a rigid working plan. These NUMBERS are a guide to your personal minimum standard. Meaning, even though you exceed your quota, you should never settle for less than your quota.

This approach to your NUMBERS also applies to the amount of time you spend on the phone. Take note of how many calls you've made within your desired time, and take note of how many of those calls are successful and how many are not.

This will allow you to adjust your sales process accordingly and therefore finding the perfect balance of how much time you spend to make money.

Numbers you need to keep an eye on are, your LEAD NUMBERS, PROSPECT NUMBERS, and your SALES NUMBERS.

Lead numbers

This is the number of leads you have on any given day, week, month or year. To keep a consistent flow of sales, this number needs to be replenished through lead referrals or marketing support.

Prospect numbers

This is the number of people you have actually spoken to and had the chance to present your offer in full. The more people you speak to, the better your chances of success.

Sales numbers

This is the number of actual sales accepted by your prospects and confirmed with banking details or cash payments. REMEMBER, a promise to pay or to accept does not count as a sale. A sale is an order accepted and confirmed with payment or banking details.

Other Numbers – cancellations, returns, and non-payment

Your success in the call center is based primarily on the number of sales you make. More than that, your success will also be influenced by the number of loyal customers who stay on your books. It's not just about the number of sales you make, but also the number of sales you keep.

The function of "KEEPING"customers may be tasked to a different department like client care or retentions. Remember, losing a customer you've worked hard to convince will affect your numbers as well.

Cancellations, returns, and non-payments may seem like irrelevant numbers but they have great influence on your success.

Understanding how many cancellations, returns and non-payments you get will help you improve how you sell and position your product.

If your cancellations are high, think about adding loyalty inducing words in your script. With all my life insurance clients, I always make a point to mention that "life cover is not something you buy today and cancel tomorrow because you got a better offer."

I say this if the client asks about our cancellation policy or mentioned they wanted to compare my price to that of our competitor. Later when we unpack the WINNING SUCCESS FORMULA, you will learn about anticipating responses and handling objections.

Know Your Ratios

With every call you make, and every prospect you speak to and the number of sales you make, soon enough these numbers start to show a pattern. This pattern is called a ratio.

Remember the 50:30:5 ratio I spoke about, if you keep to a simple number that works for you, soon you'll start to have a SUCCESS PATTERN.

With this number becoming a habit, a pattern starts to emerge. Your success becomes consistent because you have stuck to a ratio that is consistent and habitual.

Average call center salespeople don't know their numbers, let alone where these numbers come from.

If you still don't get why your numbers are important, later on, I will show you how adding two or 5 more calls could increase or double your income in a week, in a month and in a year.

You may not be able to talk to 20 more prospects in a day but if you were able to speak to an additional 2 people a day, by the end of the week you would have spoken to 10 more people.

Keeping with the same ratio of 50:30:5 it's clear to see that if you speak to 30 people in a day you would get 5 sales; By adding 5 more leads or speaking to 3 more people a day, the NUMBERS start to change which would translate to a weekly number of 25 leads and 15 more people spoken to.

With 3 more prospects per day, your sales ratio starts looking something like this - a daily ratio 55:33:6. At the end of the week, your number will be 275:165:30.

By adding 5 more leads and speaking to just 3 more people a day you could end up with 5 more sales by the end of the week.

5 more sales that you would NOT have if you just stuck to your normal performance.

As a rule of thumb, the following ratios are just as important:

Lead to Prospect ratio

This ratio is an indication of how many people you have spoken to and had the chance to present your product in full versus the number of leads you have.

You may not have control of this NUMBER because it depends on whether or not the leads you call actually give you the opportunity to talk to them about your product or service.

If you had 20 leads and you were only able to speak to 15 prospects then you ratio would look something like this 20:15 or 75%.

Depending on your lead source this would be an indicator of how reliable your lead source is and if your number is low, this is where you need to think out of the box and get referrals from the prospects you speak to.

Lead to Sale Ratio = CONVERSION

This is a good indicator of how well you turn your leads into sales. This is what many in sports call a strike rate. The number of times you score for every attempt you take. With improved skills and knowledge on how to better understand your client's NEEDS, how to better communicate the benefits of your product and how to sell like a SUPERSTAR, your LEAD-TO-SALE ratio improves.

To achieve greater success in sales, this is a ratio to maintain, to improve and also to learn from.

To give you an idea on how to increase your CONVERSION rate, accept that it comes with experience, unlike the Lead to Prospect ratio which you have little control over, LEAD TO SALE is not out of your control.

It requires a great deal of learning and knowledge to maintain or improve it.

With a better understanding of your client's NEEDS, being able to ask the right questions and offer the relevant benefits, this number will turn those sales that you MIGHT GET into sales you MUST GET.

How to Double Your Income?

Remember at the beginning of the book, I mentioned you have 3 kinds of sales available at your disposal - the SALE YOU WANT, the SALE YOU CAN'T GET (no matter what your price is) and the SALE YOU MUST GET.

Doubling your income works on the same principle - 1 in 3 sales is yours for the taking. You don't have to do much work for it, if you say the right things about your product, you prospect will buy.

If you're working in an outbound skill set, the client was probably looking for the product or service you're offering and you just happened to call at the right time. The second 1 in 3 sales is the SALE that was never yours from the beginning.

The last 1 in 3 sales is the SALE you'll need to prepare for. Your prospect will need convincing you're the right service provider for their NEED or problem, and the SALES SUPERSTAR WINNING FORMULA is designed to help you win this last 1 in 3 sales.

Back to the question on how you can double your income now that you know you're able to convert 2 in 3 sales, with these 3 ways you can increase your income by simply doing a little bit extra:

1. *More Calls More Often*

I'm always amazed at how people working in the call center find the time to chat, play games or be on their mobile phone. I am well aware of the fact that to succeed, one needs to rest and break from routine from time to time.

The fact that you're working in a call center should say something about what activity should occupy a great deal of your time – CALLING.

The fact that you are in SALES means more than anything, you should be SELLING. The one way to double your income is to speak to more people in the same amount of time. As with the ratios on Leads to Prospect, doubling your income means calling 5 or more leads than you would normally do.

As you saw with the Lead to Prospect Ratio, just speaking to 3 more people a day would mean 15 more potential buyers by the end of the week. Using the same example as with the Lead to Prospect numbers, an additional sale a day could mean 5 more sales per week; with that, your income could increase by 20 more sales in a month.

2.   *More Sales More Often*

As mentioned before, this NUMBER is well within your control. To get better at closing, read more about closing techniques, try them out, keep what works and let go of whatever doesn't work.

Selling is a skill that can be learned. With practice, we become better at what we practice more often.

Use the skills in this book, learn what other successful salespeople are doing and incorporate that into your sales process.

Imagine if you are currently closing on 5 sales of the 50 leads you get, how much more profitable would you be if you closed an additional 2 more because you asked the right questions, offered the relevant solution and were persistent by not taking the first "No" for an answer.

3.   *More Revenue per Sale*

I've worked in many call centers, most of my work has been in the insurance industry, everything from car and household insurance, to funeral and now life insurance.

With every product, I know I can always up sell my prospect with an additional benefit which always means more premiums or more revenue per sale.

To illustrate my point, while on the phone with a client that was looking for Life Insurance for her home loan, something that's become standard practice with every home loan application. In our conversation about what she did for a living, she mentioned her job requires that she is on the road a majority of her working time.

At the beginning of the call she had specifically mentioned that she was only looking for Life Insurance, I then suggested to her that she top up with Disability Insurance as well.

I introduced this additional benefit to my client just as I was about to tell her what it would cost to cover her life, I said to her "Since you are on the road all the time, don't you think it would only be SMARTER to add Disability Insurance. Should you be involved in an accident, and are disabled, the last thing you should worry about is where you will get money to pay for the bond?" then I kept quiet and waited for her response.

After a short while the response came, "How much more would that cost me?" I said, "at most, the price of a burger and coke" making it something she can relate to. To which she said, "Ok, let's hear the price and we can go ahead."

It would have been easy to sell ONLY on what she wanted, being more suggestive about the additional benefit, I was able to increase her premium by more than 20% of the initial price. Selling more to the same client is simple when you know how.

Ask the right questions and offer relevant additional benefits to increase your revenue per client.

Go the extra mile

The difference between an ORDINARY call center sales agent and the EXTRAordinary SALES SUPERSTAR is just that little bit EXTRA.

When I started in call center sales, I only had to work from 8am to 4:30pm and occasionally we had to come in on weekends. This was standard. One day I decided to stay a little after work for about an hour more than my usual working hours; in that EXTRA hour of work, I made an additional sale.

This might not seem like anything great, after all, it is just one more sale, but it was one more sale than I had made on any other day.

From that day, I make the habit of staying at least an hour more than my usual time at least 3 times in a week, and that has made all the different.

Later on in my life, when I moved closer to my workplace, on the occasional Saturday when I really had nothing to do, instead of sitting around watching television, I would pop into the office, make a couple of calls, never more than 2 hours and that also changed my INCOME in a big way.

I got more practice on the phone, so I closed more sales. I spoke to more people than the average sales agent and that meant more prospects and eventually more sales.

All it takes is that little bit EXTRA.

SUPERSTAR SALES success does not require too much. It's not about breaking your back to work a 12 hour day. Being a SALES SUPERSTAR just means you're ready and willing to do the things that others won't because you want to have what other don't.

Learning how to close better, being a little bit more persistent after the first 'No'. Calling one extra lead just before you knock off, or going that extra mile to put in an additional hour every other day you get a chance.

That's all it takes.

There's really nothing special about any other person in your call center, the only difference is that the SALES SUPERSTAR is ready and willing to go that EXTRA MILE.

Are you?

***

The Sales Superstar Winning Formula

"No matter how good you are, you're going to lose one-third of your games. No matter how bad you are you're going to win one-third of your games. It's the other third that makes the difference."

– Tommy Lasorda

Chapter 6

THE WINNING SALES FORMULA

Believe it or not, success has a pattern.

Some people attribute their success to luck or some kind of inheritance, I like to think you make your own luck and you inherit the choices you make.

Before I can tell you what the SALES SUPERSTAR WINNING FORMULA is really about, you need to understand , to be successful, you've got to say, think and do things other successful people say, think and do.

In call center sales, it is no different.

When I started in sales, I made the same mistakes every other person starting in the call center makes.

I was in a rush to make money fast, I never stopped to think about how to do it right the first time.

Sharpen Your Skills

Many years ago my uncle told me a story about how two Tree Loggers were hired to cut down trees.

On the morning when the two were scheduled to start their job, the instruction was simple, the more trees you cut down the more money you get paid.

The one Logger eager to get started got in early picked up his axe and straight into the woods he went and started chopping on trees.

His partner on the other hand also came in early to get started but instead of heading straight for the woods he took some time to prepare his axe with a sharpening stone while planning his approach.

Each time he would go into the woods, he made a point of taking some time to break and return to sharpening his axe. At the end of the day when their employer returned to pay his hard working employees. The first Tree Logger showed his employer the number of tree stumps to indicate the number of trees he had cut down.

His employer took stock, counted and confirmed, "You have done a great job" he said, "You have 10 trees down." 10 gold coins were handed to him.

The second Tree Logger presented his pile of trees and counting the number of tree stumps, his employer confirmed he had 3 more trees than the other Tree Logger. "13 trees down, great work." and 13 gold coins were handed to him.

"I have to ask," said his employer, "how did you manage more trees. Each time I came to check up on you, you seemed more concerned about sharpening your axe than you were about cutting down trees."

His response is the true essence of what it means to be a SALES SUPERSTAR.

The Tree Logger who had cut down more trees said: "Before I started I wanted to make sure my axe was sharp enough for me to cut faster, better and quicker."

He added "And whenever I felt my Axe was blunt and not cutting as effective as I wanted, I would go back to the sharpening stone to make it sharper"

Coaching and Learning

I took this lesson into my next call center job. In my first week after product training, while everyone who was in the same training as I was on the floor making sales, I was spending time with top sales advisors, listening to their recorded calls and learning how they do it so I could do the same or better.

With every top sales advisor, I realised there's something about how they take the client through the sales process.

I was good with over the phone sales, but they were better and I wanted to be better than they were. I became aware of the similarities they shared which made them special; a SUPERSTAR kind of special.

There was really nothing different about them when you compare them to the average sales advisor, but what they did differently is that they afforded EXTRAordinary attention to the following - Cultivating their personalities, learning and understating who they are selling to, studying their product in depth and working with a simple yet proven method of delivering the sales message.

I came to understand this EXTRAordinary success boils down to 4 simple principles:

1. Knowing yourself

2. Knowing your client

3. Knowing your product

4. Mastering the process (of delivering the sales message)

KNOW YOURSELF

I've equated the work of a call center sales agent to that of movie stars and movie superheroes, more specifically I like to think of them as the "Superman" and "Superwoman" of sales.

Think of Clark Kent and Superman, the same person, ordinary to the naked eye and superhero to those in need of his help. Rescuing your clients in a time of need is every bit a part of every CALL CENTER AGENT's job.

As a superhero, you need to know your powers and your weaknesses, with the aim of stretching the limits of your powers and limiting the exposure of your weaknesses.

Know Your Strengths and Weaknesses

Know your strengths as well as weaknesses. You need to know what skills work in your favor and use those as much as you can, but also know what skills you may lack and see how you can compliment them or limit their use.

After all, it would be foolish for Superman to walk into a room full of kryptonite when he knows that's his weakness.

Movies stars have made us believe in superheroes, we cannot forget they are human as they play a role of fulfilling our need and desire to believe in someone that's out to protect us.

There's a common thought among successful people: "When you know who you are, you'll know what you want. When you know what you want, you can set in motion actions in the direction of whatever you want to achieve."

In the call center, YOU are your best tool. Knowing how to use 'YOU' to get the best result means you achieve better results easier and faster.

Knowing who YOU are, lets you know what to change to get better results. If you know yourself to be charming and articulate in your words, use your charm because you know how to say the right things to get the sale.

The key to unlocking the value of your products, services or benefits is to understand how VALUE-ABLE your PERSONALITY is to the SALES process.

So What Makes a Sales Superstar?

When I think about what makes a SALES SUPER-STAR, I am reminded of a story about a young Jehovah's Witness disciple.

Every morning he would walk the neighborhood knocking on doors to talk to people all in the name of spreading the Gospel.

This one particular house had very big and vicious dogs that would rip you to pieces if they got hold of you. Each morning when he walked up to the gate of this one house, the vicious dogs would start barking hysterically.

As he stood at the gate he noted there was always someone peeping through the window but never bothered to come to the gate to attend to whatever he had to say.

This went on for a while.

One day the house owner came out to the gate screaming at the top of his voice, over the loud sounds of his barking dogs. "Why do you keep coming back when clearly you can see I am not attending to you?"

In response, the young man said, "Sir, I believe in what I want to share with you, and until you tell me you are not interested, I will keep coming back?"

This story is everything a SALES SUPERSTAR should be - believing in what you do:

1. *Attitude*

Attitude is everything. Think of CALL CENTER SALES as a special case of insanity, doing the same thing over and over again expecting a different, if not better result.

Having the right attitude to compete with yourself and others and still come out on top consistently time and time again. You'll need the right attitude to keep going. Many people lose heart and give up before they get to glory.

By keeping your spirits up and maintaining a smile throughout the day, surely you will have more positive interactions with customers.

It also makes your days all the more enjoyable.

It is no wonder every call center tries to keep spirits up with games, chants and songs to keep the fire going. Have a good attitude. Have a genuine interest in helping other people. Most of all keep smiling even on a cloudy day.

2. Persistence

With every CALL you have one of two CHOICES. You can give up or you can keep trying. Being able to handle one rejection after another and still be able to pick up the phone and try again, this is the true essence of a SALES SUPERSTAR.

You'll have good days, and you'll have bad days. Continue to do what you do best and that will see you through many more sales.

Your prospects will tell you time and time again how they are "Not Interested", but when you believe in yourself, your company and your products, surely every 'NO' is just one step closer to a 'YES'.

SALES SUPERSTARS are persistent in their quest for getting the sale. Don't give up. Some clients will call you PUSHY, or 'TOO SALESY' or maybe drop the call on you. Persistently stand for what you believe in, your client is better off with your product.

Keep asking the right questions, keep getting the commitment and always KEEP MOVING THE SALES PROCESS FORWARD to the close.

3. *Urgency*

Whoever said good things come to those who wait must have died waiting before correcting their thoughts.

Successful SALES SUPERSTARS have a sense of urgency about getting things done, while focusing on the goal - offering what your client WANTS, VALUES and can COMMIT TO - closing the sale.

You could potentially be following up on pending deals for the rest of your life while other people are closing on the first day. In the call center, unlike with face to face sales, you only have one shot and only one shot to make or break a sale. Every day a sale is not closed, the chances of closing that sale reduce exponentially by the day. This is especially true for products and services where your clients can make a decision on the spot, like insurance or mobile phone contracts or extended car warranty.

Without a sense of URGENCY, you'll always be chasing the pending deal instead of closing sales; and this is not to say you should not 'follow through' on legitimate pending deals, but never leave pending a sale that would have otherwise been closed.

4. *Candour*

Sales Superstars possess a great amount of frankness and brutal honesty. There is no "SUGAR COATING" of why your client needs your product.

Besides, your brutal honesty will show off as confidence in yourself, your product and your company. There is nothing more attractive to your clients than confidence all round.

Your 'No' should be an 'NO', your 'Yes' should be a 'YES'. When your client is making an ill-informed decision, be the first to call out and tell your client they are making a BIG mistake. They might not like you for it, but they will surely respect and appreciate that you care enough to be honest about what you can and cannot do for them.

5. *Listening*

The greatest skill you can have as a CALL CENTER AGENT is the skill of listening; not just listening to what is being said but also what is not being said.

You would that in an environment where you get paid to speak to clients, you should be doing more talking and less listening. The opposite is true.

SALES SUPERSTARS possess the ability to ask the right questions and be able to listen for the right buying signals.

After all the purpose of every call is not just to talk to your prospects but to get them to buy your product, and listening is the key to getting more sales.

REMEMBER, there's a good reason why you have two ears and one mouth – to listen twice as much as you talk.

6. *Commitment*

Commitment is about taking a stand for what you believe in, seeing the process through, taking the responsibility and the resolution to give your best.

Commitment is about making and keeping a promise to be the best that your client can expect and more.

Not every client will be the same. Irrespective of the call, make the commitment to service every client with same awesomeness anytime and every time. I find it strange when call center sales agents become rude to the client on the phone because they have a pre-conceived idea about the client's needs, wants and affordability.

Commit to the process.

7. *Motivation*

More importantly, SELF MOTIVATION. Let's call this the 'WHY'. 'Why do you do what you do?'

It's easy to say, SELLING is just about making money. To be honest, money is everything and should never be taken for granted; some people might say they don't care much for money.

Even if that's the case, I can sure bet my SALARY, there's always something that motivates 'WHY' they do what they do. When I was young, I didn't have much. I can remember the one time when we went to bed having had only tea and a slice of bread for supper.

I've since found that having money means I can have anything I want, eat out when I want, travel when I want and pretty much do as I please because I am not restricted by how much I have or don't have.

Whatever motivates you, maybe it is the prospect of a new car, a house of your own, new shoes and clothes every month, providing for your family or recognition among friends, family, and colleagues.

Whatever your MOTIVATION, you will get further with SELF MOTIVATION than if you had no MOTIVE to achieve anything at all.

Having the motivation to succeed is the reason 'WHY' you want to be a SALES SUPERSTAR. Whatever your reason for being in SALES, let that driving force be constantly available to you.

I know many call center sales agents who keep a picture of their family, a car they desire or a house they want to buy as a reminder and motivation for what they do. I do the same, I have a picture of my lovely wife to remind me why I do what I do.

Whatever the reason, remember, all successful SALES SUPERSTAR have the motivation to start, to strive and to succeed at whatever they do.

KNOW YOUR CLIENT

We make assumptions about our clients. Whether we are calling them or they called us, we still make assumptions. You know what they say about ASSUMPTIONS, "it's making an ass(et) out of me and you."

Cliché but true.

The only assumption about your client should be based on your expectations of the sales call, "The client has a need or desire, and if you are able to satisfy or fulfill that need or desire", 'EXPECT' the client to buy from you. ASSUME the sale.

Call center sales is a little bit like speed dating.

Whatever your thoughts are about the concept of speed dating let me share the similarities that make selling in the call center all the more fun. For those of you who have no idea what speed dating is because your GAME is really good, let me school you a little.

According to a speed dating website, speed dating is basically an opportunity to meet and date 12-15 people, who are serious about wanting to be in a relationship.

You will date each person for about five minutes, giving you the opportunity to decide if you want to see that person again. Why is this similar to call center sales?

Depending on what skill set you are working – inbound or outbound, every day you will speak to 10 to 15 people who have a need, at most your call will be anything from 20min to about 45min to give you the opportunity to decide if you want to see them again.

The last part about "...giving you the opportunity to decide if you want to see them again." can be a little confusing for a lot of call center agents. I disagree with the idea that clients choose us and not the other way around. I like to think that I CHOOSE my clients.

To give you a little bit of insight into how to make your sales call all the most successful, remember the following, which by the way work well in speed dating:

1. *Focus on the person you're talking with, not on the impression you're making.*

2. *Be interested in them, and they'll be more likely to be interested in you.*

3. *Keep it light and fun; take nothing personally.*

4. *Be prepared for almost anything. Some people come with questions, be prepared to answer honestly and frankly.*

5. *Be yourself.*

Going back to the speed dating analogy, call center sales is different in that you are not able to see your client. You have no basis for making a judgment call on the way they look, stand or walk.

All you have is a voice and the information they give to you, which you take at face value. Just as much as the client will know you by the way you speak, the words you use and the energy you put into delivering an outstanding performance, expect to know your clients by the same qualities.

Know your client's voice.

Your client's voice is the face of your entire sales conversation. Listening to your client and internalizing what they say is the eye contact of the sale.

I find that asking questions is the foundation of getting to know your client, and therefore, ask as many basic questions as possible to have enough information about your client to help you make an informed presentation.

As I mention earlier, your client will always respond in kind; and when they do respond in kind then you know your client is open to your advice.

More than just knowing your client's voice and expressions, the following knowledge of your client will greatly increase your number of sales and improve the rate at which you turn your prospects into SALES.

Know your client's name

Picture yourself in a room full of people and someone was screaming your name. That would make you stop to look around for the person calling you by name. If your name was said with such familiarity, you would definitely respond in kind - seeing who is calling your name.

The same principle applies to clients on the phone, call them by name. Regardless of what product you are selling, I believe the client would respond better to "Good morning John..." more than they would to "Good Morning Mr. John Smith."

Respect always goes a long way. That said, you need to understand how much calling your client by name gives you authority to speak as equals.

I've had men and women respond with "Yes sir..." on the phone simply because I called them by name and therefore identified with me as a valued advisor and equal in stature. Clients never ask me my age and depending on who I am speaking to I will adapt my use of words and mannerisms to suit the situation.

After all, that is what successful movie stars do, they fit into the script. As a rule of thumb, always call your clients by their first name, unless they tell you to refer to them as "Mr. Smith." in which case you need to upgrade to their level and refer to yourself as "Mr. Sales Person".

Don't get this wrong. I have seen many call center sales people who take the low ground in the conversation, which does nothing for positioning them as the AUTHORITY and EXPERT in their field, product or service.

It is fair and well to refer to your client by "Sir" or "Madam" as a sign of respect, however, the key to being in control of the conversation is to always call your client by their first name. This may go against your culture or upbringing, but you need to know, in the world of business unless you are prepared to play as equals, you are always going to be on the losing end.

Know your client's language

I grew up speaking slang – the kind of language my English teacher would cringe if she ever heard me use it in public.

In the world of CALL CENTER SALES, you'll come across a range of people, some will be very formal, some will be very commanding and some will be very polite and friendly. Irrespective of who you're selling to, treat your clients all the same - without judgment.

Successful SALES SUPERSTARS know how to talk to their clients irrespective of their position, income, gender or qualification.

At the end of the day, the objective is to get a sale and for your client to get a solution to their problems or the relief to their pain.

As a starting point, I suggest going neutral in your language. Not too formal, not too casual. Just being you unless being you is anything other than desirable.

Once you have familiarized yourself with your client, lean towards connecting with the client at a level they can relate to. Pay attention to the words used by your client.

This is what I like to refer to as the mirror effect. If the client says "I am looking for the perfect holiday destination..." then you respond by saying "I will find you the PERFECT holiday destination."

This also applies when you're selling other products, like insurance; whatever the client says to describe their problem, use the same words to describe the solution.

So when your client says "I am looking for life cover to protect my children's future..." you mirror that, your solution needs to be "This cover is designed to PROTECT your children's future...".

Know your client's pain point

Parting with money is not an easy thing to do especially when you have worked hard to earn it. However, as much as people hate to be sold to, they actually love to buy. Your job as a SALES SUPERSTAR is to assist your prospects with their buying decision.

The only way I know how to do that is to make your product and or service more valuable than the price they have to pay.

Think of car insurance; your prospects are not buying just car insurance, they are buying the peace of mind knowing that should anything happen, be it an accident or a theft, they have someone who will replace their valuable mode of transport with ease and hustle free.

Take it one step back. Think of the client buying a car, they are not necessarily just buying a mode of transport to get them from point A to point B.

What they are looking for is the comfort and control of when to move, whenever they wish to move.

Understanding your client's pain point simply means understanding what they are willing to exchange in return of avoiding that POINT OF PAIN.

With physical products you can touch and feel; it may be easy to put into perspective but not so with intangible products.

Take away your client's car and see how they react to using unreliable public transport.

Take away the comfort of knowing they're not sharing their seat in the car with anyone, and they are in control of when to move, whenever they wish to move. Then you will see how soon your prospects are willing to exchange whatever money they have to return to a point of comfort and control.

This may be a bit difficult with services you cannot see, touch or feel. In that case, you need to paint pictures that are so vivid your prospects can almost see, touch and feel.

For many prospects, the price would seem like their only pain point, for others, it may be their families, their comfort, their joy or their happiness.

Remember! People buy products as services for one of two reasons, either to eliminate pain or to increase pleasure.

While selling may be a logical process, buying is an emotional decision. Know what EMOTIONS connect to their NEEDS and DESIRES, only then will you know what really motivates their buying decisions.

I can remember one client who called in looking for life cover (also known as life insurance). She had been to a funeral and the widow had expressed concern her husband had left very little financial provisions in the event of his death.

After many years of being a homemaker, she now had to go back to looking for a job so she could continue paying for the home loan and other household expenses. With that, I knew her POINT OF PAIN; the uncertainty of the future in the event of death.

Affordability is something we all consider when buying something we value, my job was to make my product more valuable to eliminating her 'Pain' of an uncertain future than the price she had to pay.

Talking about how I (or 'We' as the company) would hate to put her in the same position as her friend's husband, I gave her the peace of mind in knowing we will be there for her.

This goes deeper than just getting a sale, but knowing what you have to offer is the real solution to the problem your client has.

If it means touching on the painful points to get your client BUYING, you would have done a great job, because you would have saved a family from destitute, or you would have provided a client with a new car, had their car been stolen.

Know your prospect's pain point. If it is price, save them money; be innovative, if you can, offer a discount or repackage your offer to make it affordable by lowering the amount of cover, removing benefits or changing pricing structure.

Always reassure the client that what you have to offer is the best they can afford. When they are in a better financial position, they can upgrade their package. If it is about providing for their family, paint the picture of what it would be like for a widow without the financial provisions of their spouse. Finding your client's 'pain point' should not be difficult and intrusive to your selling process. When doing your needs assessment, ask about their needs and desires; for instance, when I sell life insurance, I always ask my clients why they're looking for life insurance.

If they say they are looking for a comparative price, then I know their 'Pain Point' is most likely price. If they say they want to get Life Cover so that when death does come, their loved one are provided for.

Then I know the need to provide for their loved ones is the 'PAIN POINT'.

Always probe a little further, if their PAIN POINT seems vague; ask questions such as "Are you married?" "Any kids, how old are they?" "Is it boys or girls?" Where the point of pain is not evident, create it. Where there seems to be NO NEED, create it.

There is always a need, you just need to find it and find the point of pain to your client's NEED. Know your prospect's POINT OF PAIN and you have certainly have a sale if the solution is right.

Know your client's level of commitment

At the beginning of every call, I like to know my prospect's commitment to the conclusion of a sale. Later on, when I talk about your product, you will understand why it is important to know your client's commitment from the beginning of the conversation. To assess commitment, I normally ask the question, "When you are HAPPY with what I have to offer you, when do you want to start, immediately or at the end of the month?"

This might not be possible for every product or service, or even with every prospect but you are better off knowing than speculating on your client's commitment. Imagine a marathon runner preparing for a big race. If the runner has no expectation or knowledge of what they will face on the run, how are they to prepare for what to expect.

Your client needs to know that should they be HAPPY with what you have to offer, they have to make a decision and commit to a solution. As you will later learn in the "SALES SUPERSTAR Tips and Tactics", knowing your client's level of commitment also prepares you for what to expect throughout the selling process.

For example, when a client says "I am not sure when to start." You know you will have to create a sense of urgency over and above their sense of need for your product or service. If the client says "I can only start in 3 months time."

Then you know to probe why and work out how you can get your prospect to commit to a date sooner than they planned.

Find out what your client will commit to in terms of price, value and benefits. Pose questions to your prospects that will reveal their commitment to start dates and loyalty to the company you represent.

Never be afraid to ask questions like "So when do you want your benefits to start?" "How long do you want to have these benefits for?"

I used to ask my car insurance clients, how long they were with their previous insurer, or what insurance company their parents use or used.

This gives me the idea of how long they intend to stay with us, and whether they have the same sense of loyalty as their parents.

As you would know, many people are loyal to the brands their parents are loyal to.

Know Your Product

If I asked you what product the McDonald's franchise sells, would you know? Even better, do you know what product is sold by the Coca-Cola Company? If you said burgers for McDonald's and soda for Coca-Cola, you would be wrong. McDonald's sells conveniently located fast food and the Coca-Cola Company sells refreshments.

Still don't get it? Read on, I will explain.

When I sell to my clients, irrespective of the solution i.e. Insurance, Holiday Package or Cellphone Contract, my product is "HAPPINESS", happiness with what I have to offer.

Some people sell 'LOGIC', others sell 'SAVINGS' for example, "If I can save you an X amount of money on your current phone bill, would you start your contract immediately or at the end of the month?"

This ties back to getting your prospect's commitment from the start of the sales process.

A lot of company training for new recruits focuses on solutions training - often referred to as PRODUCT TRAINING; what I am talking about here is not that kind of product. This is not to say knowledge about your 'SOLUTION' is not important. In fact, it is very important. However, you need to know YOUR PROD-

UCT over and above whatever solution your company has hired you to sell.

To give you an idea of what I am talking about. The following is what would happen between myself and the prospect over the phone:

Me: "So tell me John, when you are HAPPY with what I have to offer you, when are you looking to start your cover, immediately or at the end of the month?"

Prospect: "... End of the month."

Me: "And on what date do you normally get paid."

Prospect: "On the last day of the month."

Me: "So can we run your order/payment from the 1st of the month?'

Prospect: "That would be fine."

See how from the beginning of the sales process, I have told my client exactly what they will be buying from me – 'HAPPINESS'. Plus I now have the commitment for when they would like to pay for their 'Happiness'.

At the end of the sales process, when I've done my presentation, I tell my client how much "HAPPINESS" will cost; simply by saying "All of this for ONLY X amount." To which I ask, "Are you HAPPY with that?"

When the prospect says "Yes, I am HAPPY", I ask for banking details and close the sale.

If there are any responses, questions or objections, I deal with them and return to the question "Are you HAPPY with that?" Again, when the client says "Yes, I am HAPPY."

I ask for banking details and close the sale.

The same applies if you decide that "Logic" is your product. In this case, you would ask the question, "It is only logical to use our product or service."

When the prospect says "Yes." You ask for banking details and close your sale.

If your product is "Savings", the question would be, "This would be a great SAVING for you."; when the client says 'YES.'

You ask for banking details and close the sale.

See how simple it is to sell when you know your PRODUCT.

With every sale that is meant to be, this will be an easy close. With every sale that was never meant to be, this will be an experience to cherish and a lesson to learn from your prospects responses and objections.

This I will deal with in the chapter on "Responses and Objections"

The one-third of sales will separate you from the rest of the pack.

MASTER THE PROCESS

Selling is a process, there's a beginning, a middle and an end. Call center sales is not any different.

The only way to get the best out of every sales call, or at least many of your sales calls, it is to master the selling process.

Every sale on the phone will have to go through the same process and it comes in four simple stages:

1. **THE SETUP**

2. **THE PROCESSING**

3. **THE PRESENTATION**

4. **THE CLOSE**

Every stage of the selling process has only one objective. And it is not to make a sale, it is not to get to more information, it is not to present your product or to close the sale, even though all these are part of the process.

The only objective you should be worried about is this – the objective of stage 1 of the sales process is to get to the second stage and the objective of the second stage is to get to the third stage and so on and so forth.

It is that simple. Don't try to complicate things by doing a presentation when you should be setting up your sale. Whatever product you're selling, know that when you start at the SETUP STAGE, the main objective is to get to the PROCESSING STAGE, that's it.

The purpose of the entire FLOW is to advance the sales cycle to the point of PRESENTATION and then CLOSING THE SALE.

The only way to know if the SETUP STAGE was done right, is if you move on to the point where the prospect is giving you information for PROCESSING, and whatever other information you'll need from them to get to the next stage – where you will be PRESENTING your product and then CLOSING THE SALE.

Whenever I pick up the phone, whether it is an incoming call or I made the call to the client. My aim is not only to close the client, my main objective is to advance the sales process to the next level; to the point where I get the information I can use to present my product.

This is very common with new call center agents, the first thing the client says to them is "Sorry, but I am not interested." Agent will respond with the outdated and silly answer: "How can you not be interested when you don't even know what I have to offer." It does nothing to advance the sales process; it simply ignites an argument with your prospect.

What you need to be saying is, "A lot of my clients initially said they were not interested until they heard what I had to offer."

What this says to the client is, he or she is not alone in "Not being interested" but your prospect can now listen to what you have to offer. This advances the sales process to the point of gathering information for PROCESSING.

Before I go into detail about the process, I hope you've understood that each stage of the process is vital and the objective of each stage it to get to the next stage, NOTHING MORE. So yes, the last stage is the CLOSING STAGE, before that is the PRESENTATION STAGE and the presentation stage only comes after the information PROCESSING STAGE which is preceded by the opening SETUP STAGE.

Get it. Good, now let's get into it.

1. The Setup

It is easy to get rushed into things when you are on the phone with your prospect. When you've had a long day and one prospect after the other keeps telling you they do not have the time to listen, it can be tempting to start your PRESENTATION when you have not even reached the presentation stage.

The name of this stage of the sales process makes it easy to relate to what you want to achieve – put in place the right elements to ensure success - SETUP FOR A SUCCESSFUL SALES CALL.

Other people might call this the opening, I call it the 'SETUP' because unless you 'SET UP' the conversation to understand what you want to offer your prospective client, your closing is as good as a fight or a battle you might not win.

With the 'SETUP', keep it simple, no gimmicks, no tricks. Be clear and straight to the point.

Simply introduce yourself to your prospect.

Remember the main objective of THE SETUP is to get you to the next stage, the information PROCESSING stage.

I find a simple "Good day, John" if I know the clients name, "You're through to the XYZ Insurance, how are you doing today?" does a great job to move the selling process into the next stage.

As a personal touch, I always follow through with a statement of appreciation. My SETUP would sound something like this:

Me: "Good day John, you're through to XYZ Insurance Company, how're you doing today."

Prospect: "I am well, how are you."

Me: "I am well. Thank you for taking my call."

This simple opening applies to either inbound or outbound skill sets, regardless of whether it is a cold call or established lead. The procedure is the same, simple and straight to the point.

REMEMBER! THE SETUP is a short conversation to QUICKLY BUILD RAPPORT with your prospective client in preparation to ask relevant questions that will help you understand how you can help them achieved their goal of increase pleasure or reduced pain.

2. The Processing Stage

At this stage, there's only one thing you need to know, and that's "What information do I have to know in order to make the right presentation."

This part of the sales cycle gets you to process the information given by your prospective client such that you are able to make an informed PRESENTATION.

As the process flows, the closing comes from the presentation and the presentation comes from the 'PROCESSED' information.

The right information will lead to the right presentation and therefore the right closing.

See how all these stages tie up to each other.

The only way to have the right information is by asking the right questions, and asking the right questions might not mean you will get the right answers but you can read between the lines of what your prospect is saying. So when the client says, I would like to get a quote, what they mean is one of many things, among which the following falls:

"I would like to compare what you have to offer to what I currently have to see if I can get a better offer." Or "I would like to know what it will cost me to solve the problem I have, alleviate the pain or increase my pleasure. If I am happy with the value I will commit."

Conventional sales training says you should never assume anything about your client. That's all good and well, but the SALES SUPERSTAR WINNING FORMULA is not conventional. If it was, I would not be writing this book.

Here's the Sales Superstar way of doing things.

The principles of processing information are contained in these two statements:

1. *Assume and verify.*

2. *Lead the way,*

The key to successful selling is finding out what people value. And knowing what people value will help you understand what they might need or want, or what problems they might have.

The sales process is for one purpose and one purpose only, to make a sale. At the beginning of the book, I mentioned there are 3 sales available to you, the sales that will be, the sale that will never be, and the sale that must be.

Gathering as much information as possible is about making sure the sales that "Must be" will be - in a way increasing your profitability. You could easily pick up the phone and say "What I am about to offer you will help you do what you do better or it will remove pain or increase pleasure."

Truth be told, you are better off saying that when you know a little bit more about your client. Ask questions about what they value, their family, their work and aspiration, and so on.

As you know your industry best. Take some time to write down some questions to will help you make a better presentation for your client.

In the industry I'm currently in, an industry I have worked in for most of my call center life – insurance, I know what questions to ask:

"Do you currently have insurance?"

"Are you married?"

"Do you have kids?"

"How old are your kids?"

"What work do you do?"

"How much are you currently paying?"

"How much can you afford?"

I ask these questions because I know they will give me the kind of information I need to do my presentation. Not all these questions need to be asked, however I always make it a point to ask a minimum of three or four questions.

Remember asking the right questions is the key to extracting the right information. With the right information for PROCESSING, the right kind of presentation will be done to get the sale.

When I started in sales, I went home every afternoon and wrote down possible questions I could ask a client to get the right information. Over the years, I fine tuned these questions to the point where they are almost second nature to me.

Do the same and you will find your questioning technique getting better.

This stage is probably the longest stage in the sales process and should never be rushed. The more you know about your client, the better your PRESENTATION and the easier it will be to close your sale.

PRINCIPLE #1: Assume and Verify

With the PROCESSING of information, I refer to an unconventional way of asking questions that make the SALES SUPERSTAR all the more successful.

To illustrate what I mean with the words Assume and Verify as well as Lead the Way. Let's start off with the principle of ASSUME AND VERIFY. One of the greatest mistakes made by many new CALL CENTER SALES AGENTS is trying to be TOO POLITE. Don't get it? That's fine! Allow me to explain.

At the beginning of the call you ask the question 'Is this a good time to talk.' Pause. What do you think the response will be? One of two, 'NO' or 'What is this about' or any variation of the above.

The principle of ASSUME AND VERIFY works like this. Whenever I call a prospective client, if they pick up the call, I ASSUME they are willing to talk to me.

I VERIFY by continuing with the sales process unless the client stops me by saying "This is not a good time to talk, can you call me later." Simple to understand right, ...riiight.

With the INFORMATION PROCESSING STAGE, I apply the same principle.

Whenever I ask a client a question I assume the result will move the sales process into the next stage.

Take the following call for example:

Me: "Thank you for submitting your details for us to assist you with your Car Insurance. Tell me? Do you currently have Car Insurance?"

Based on the above statement, I ASSUME that the client submitted a request because they have a car. I assume they want car insurance and verify with a question

"Do you have car insurance?"

Whatever the response, either way, the sales process will move forward.

Prospective Client: "Yes, I would like to change my Car Insurance." Or "No I do not have car insurance."

Either way, the sales process moves forward. Get the picture? I'm sure you do. In fact, I ASSUME you do and move on.

PRINCIPLE #2: Lead the Way

The principle of Leading the Way is based on the power of suggestion. Clients don't like to be told what to do or what options to choose. Nobody likes to be told what to do with their money. With enough experience you will know how to react to the different responses you will get from different clients.

A client calls in to say, "I am looking to compare pricing," lead the way towards the road of least cost.

A client looking for value, lead the way towards the road of more value. Simple enough to understand? I Assume so, but allow me to verify with a brief explanation.

If I TOLD you eating vegetables is good for you. Would that make you eat more vegetables?

Probably not!

But if I SUGGESTED that eating vegetables may be good for you especially if you are looking to lose some weight since you mentioned you wanted to lose a couple of kilos.

Chances are you may consider my suggestion because the suggestion was relevant and directed at what you wanted to achieve. The same applies to the call center sales. Take the following sales call for example:

Me: "Sir, as you mentioned to me that you had an accident before, and that left you without a car for a whole week, don't you think you would be better off with the added benefit of a car hire?"

Noticed how the above suggestion is not just a blank suggestion, it is relevant to what the client wanted to achieve or avoid in this case. It might add premium, but this is not the place to discuss it.

Me: "Option 1 is the cheapest, option 2 is more expensive than option 1, but not as expensive as option 3. Which one would you like to choose."

I use this whenever a client brings up pricing as a deciding factor in which case I lead my client towards choosing the option that will NOT cost them the most.

Every industry has its own questions to ask to help you get the right information to make a proper presentation. Take some time out to tailor your own industry-specific Information Processing questions to ask prospective clients.

3. The Presentation

A lot of sales people confuse telling with SELLING the same way they confuse a presentation with a demonstration.

To help you understand why your presentation is the ultimate key to your sales success, remember this; telling is about giving information without the expecting a decision to be made on that information.

Selling is about giving a reason why the use of whatever you're selling would benefit your client, expecting your prospect to make a buying decision. The same is true with demonstration and presentation.

While demonstration is about showcasing how your products or services work. The presentation is about giving a reason why your products or services will work for your prospect; once again expecting the prospect to make a buying decision.

With the INFORMATION you have gathered in your information PROCESSING STAGE, with an understanding of your clients pain points.

Your presentation should not just provide your prospects with information on the benefits of what you have to offer but also why you are the best solution to their problem or the only provider to their needs, wants and desires - expect a buying decision.

Your presentation needs to be alive with animation and sound. Think of it as the climax of your showcase or the epicenter of your value proposition.

Depending on your personality, and 'YOUR PRODUCT' your presentation needs to leave your prospect wondering why they are only finding out about your product now. In the chapter on the application of the 'WINNING FORMULA,' I detail how you need to project your voice for clarity, also how to project confidence and passion and how to build on likability and loyalty with every word you say.

4. The Close

Earlier I mentioned that the objective of every stage in the sales process is one, and only one – to get the sales process moving forward into the next stage.

The objective of stage 1 of the selling process is simply to get to stage 2 of the process. REMEMBER the objective of every stage is to get to the next stage, so it only makes sense that after your PRESENTATION you will be CLOSING.

In sales, there was a philosophy used by many of the successful sales agents in the call center where I worked. This philosophy is based on the acronym ABC – Always Be Closing.

I love the idea of always-be-closing, with every word you say, and every action you take, begin with the end in mind – the close. Remember, do not be so consumed by THE CLOSE you neglect gathering enough information to do a proper presentation and eventually a 'SUPERSTAR CLOSING'.

I've seen and heard many call center sales agents who OPEN with passion, GATHER INFORMATION with curious anticipation and PRESENTING with so much flair and still not close the sale.

Half the time it is not because the sales agents does not want the sale but because they fear rejection and never ask for the sale.

With the SALES SUPERSTAR WINNING FORMULA, when you know YOUR PRODUCT it is much simpler to get the sale. Open with confirmation on what your prospect is buying – Your Product (Happiness, Savings or Logic). Gather the appropriate information you'll need to do your presentation.

Do a great PRESENTATION of your offering and simply close like a "SUPERSTAR" by saying, "Are you Happy with that?" or "Does that sound like a great SAVING?" that's it.

When your prospect says "Yes", ask for banking details and close your sale. This is so much MORE EFFECTIVE than many other closing tricks I have heard used on the call center floor.

Once you understand how the SALE SUPERSTAR WINNING FORMULA works, you will be closing many more of that one-third of sales you must be closing anyway. So, remember, open with confirmation on commitment i.e. "Sir, if you are HAPPY with what I have to offer you, when do you want to start you cover?"

Gather the relevant information to make your presentation; never make the mistake of presenting before you have enough information, close by simply offering 'YOUR PRODUCT'

"Are you HAPPY with that?"

The only viable solution to your client's needs wants and desires. If the response is "YES", ASSUME the sale and ask for banking details.

***

"Winning takes talent, to repeat takes character."
– John Wooden

Chapter 7

APPLYING THE WINNING FORMULA

Success is a process, not an event. With time, you accept there's no short cut to success. The so-called overnight successes have had many years in the making.

We live in a world of fast food and takeaway. The temptation to rush success is something every call center sales agent would like to achieve.

The key to true SUPERSTAR SALES SUCCESS is understanding that reaching target one month and missing it the following month is not a formula for success - it's called 1-Hit-Wonder.

Consistency is what you are looking for.

Learn how to consistently deliver the same message with the same amount of enthusiasm and achieve the same or better results. Tweak your approach, delivery, and style. Keep what works and let go of what doesn't. That way you are continuously improving.

I have made a lot of money in the call center, but I must confess it did not all happen overnight. It took many days of trial and error, learning from others, incorporating my personality into what worked on the floor so that my success had a personal touch.

Success has a formula and results

Inaction is to success, what kryptonite is to Superman. In simpler terms, without taking action, your dreams, desires and aspirations, are nothing more than just dreams, desires and aspirations. The secret to success is doing what others won't so you can have what others don't. To be successful, your desire for success needs to exceed your fear of failure.

As the great Nelson Mandela put it, "Courage is not the absence of fear but actioning in the presence of fear."

When I started in the call center, there were many times I was afraid I might not make it. My thoughts would wonder, "What if I say the wrong thing?" or "What if they do not want whatever I am selling?"

The only way to overcome this fear is to play your part. Besides the person on the other side of the call will never know if this is your first time on the phone or you have been doing this for many years. The only way to convince them you know what you are doing is by being confident what you have to offer is the best solution they can find.

Confidence is the king maker of any person. Even on the first day on the phone, I would tell my clients "You are speaking to the senior advisor and I am going give you the best solution and value for your money."

This is not to say you should lie to your client, sometimes speaking prophecy to your success will give you more confidence to succeed. The formula to success:

Success = Desire + Knowledge (Action)^2

In words easy to understand if numbers or mathematics are not your thing. Success is equal to your desire to succeed, you add the knowledge of how to succeed and multiply the actions you take with an EXTRAordinary effort to the second power. As you would know, the tree is known by its fruit.

Success delivers result, and for me, I have measured my success by many things, my salary at the end of the month, the many properties I have invested in as a result of the money I have made, and the freedom to work in an environment where I can give my clients the best offer I can.

Start making more sales by applying the WINNING SUCCESS FORMULA, be recognized as the best advisor, the most improved advisor, and the most consistent advisor.

Make two more calls than you currently do, see what happens, be open and honest with your client when they say, "They want to think about it."Be frank and ask, "What is it that you want to think about." Don't be afraid to ask for that sale. After all, what is the worst that could happen, they say "No".

With every "No", you are a lot closer to a 'YES' so just keep on dialing? Keep SELLING to more people. Practice makes perfect. The more practice you get, the more perfect you become.

Unlocking Your Superstar Winning Formula

I tell people who ask me for advice on how to make more sales on the phone that personality is every bit as important as the product you are selling.

Simply put, be yourself unless yourself really sucks. Just as success has a formula, the SALES SUPERSTAR has a formula too, and it looks something like this:

(Job Skills + Selling Skills) X Personality = SALES SUPERSTAR

Earlier I mentioned, what makes any person a successful SALES SUPERSTAR has everything to do with attitude, persistence, urgency, candor, listening, commitment and motivation; all of which are a sum of your personality.

Unless you are not familiar with the laws of addition, subtraction and multiplication; it is easy to see that the MULTIPLIER to the Sales Superstar Winning Formula is your personality.

I can tell you about personality as I have done in the previous pages. However, I cannot teach you personality.

The only way you will turn any scripted sales message into a conversation is if you are able to internalize your offer and be able to deliver it as if it were part of who you are. Let out and be yourself, unless 'yourself' really sucks.

Unpacking Your SKILLS Tool Chest

Whenever I think about the SALES SUPERSTAR's tool chest I am reminded of Batman's cave with all the gadgets and tech ready to save the people of GOTHAM CITY.

Your skills tool chest is every bit a combination of your JOB SKILLS and SELLING SKILLS. Your tool chest should have everything you need to perform your duties to the best of your abilities. To better understand the difference between the two, JOB SKILLS refers to HOW you use the tools you have at your disposal.

JOB SKILLS include your knowledge of the phone and computer systems, communication systems like email, as well as your work planners and performance aid such as calculators.

SELLING SKILLS refer to your ability to apply whatever you know and have learned about selling into a process of achieving a successful sales call.

To start off, let's look at some of your JOB SKILLS tools and later unpack a selling process which defined the application of your SELLING SKILLS.

JOB SKILLS

a) Headset and phone – this is your most prized possession. Guard it well. Never say anything on the phone to your client which you would not repeat to your most respected family member.

I cannot begin to imagine how many sales agents have cut their careers short because they said something over the phone thinking they had dropped the call.

b) Email – master email etiquette and always make sure you check everything before you click send. Check your spelling and grammar. What you say and how you say it gives an impression about you, your company and your product.

If you do not pay attention to detail on what you send out via email, rest assured your clients have little reason to believe you will attend to the detail of their needs.

b) Calendar and planner – the mind is very quick to forget. Whenever you make an appointment, diaries it with notes. By all means keep to any agreed times.

Be flexible with your appointment. Rather tell a client or prospect "I will call you between 1pm and 1:15pm" than making a spot appointment you have no guarantee you'll be able to keep, especially when you are working in a call center environment.

Clients might not keep their appointment, but you must.

There are many other tools in your tool chest, like the pen, the marker, and the post-it notes, the above three are a good start to get you going.

SALES SKILLS

4-Step Sales Process

There are 4 basic elements to every SALES CALL:

1. Get attention
2. Gather information
3. Make your presentation
4. Close your sale

REMEMBER! Every step in the sales process has one objective – to get to the next step of the process; that simple, not rocket science or anything.

I'm going to cover all 4 steps in their order; something I like to call the FLOW.

Winging it? Acting without a Script.

I often hear sales people speak so confidently about their skills and how they never want to use a script.

That is very disturbing, especially because I see 'Sales' as a role we play to convince our prospects how our product will help them do what they do better or solve a problem easier and faster, or increase their level of pleasure by reducing their levels of discomfort.

Even The Best Movies Are Scripted

Have you seen a good movie lately? Did you enjoy it? That was scripted. The sales process is the same.

The only way to bring joy to your clients is by developing your script, internalizing it and delivering it in such a way that it feels natural. The same way that none of the great movies you have seen delivered a great experience but never felt scripted.

The idea of having a script is not to tie you down to something that is not workable for you. Your personality is every bit part of your WINNING FORMULA, the script is the guiding map to delivering your formula.

While delivering your script, remember the best way to sell is to listen to the responses from your prospects. Plug those into your process and deliver according to their needs. Your prospects may respond negatively or positively, but because you know what you will be saying to your client, you can plan on what responses to anticipate and how to act on them.

LISTENING to responses allows you to gather crucial information about buying signals and your script will guide you through that - especially if you're still new to the call center environment.

1. *Get Attention*

The sales profession has been buried in a negative reputation for lying, misleading and using false statements to get prospects to agree to buy their product and services.

That is because some call center sales people think they need to say something witty to get the attention of the person they are calling.

I have worked in different skills sets in the call center environment – both inbound and outbound. If you are working an inbound skill set, remember, the people calling in are looking for your help, find out what they are looking for.

In the outbound skill set, people will in general respond in kind. No one ever picks up the phone because they want to be rude and disrespectful for no reason. Your job is to open in kind, and your prospect will respond in kind.

I remember receiving a call from one of the big cell phone companies, the agent on the phone wanted to offer me a new cell phone contract. After introducing himself, he asked, *"Mr. Pearlal, would you be interested in a contract phone."* I responded in kind *"No".*

My response was in kind, I was honest in saying 'I am not interested' in a new contract phone package.

Remember the purpose of every stage or step of the sales process is to move the sales process forward.

The only way of achieving the objective of getting to the next stage or step of the process is to use a statement that will draw a response from your prospect in the direction of moving the sales process forward.

My response to the agent on the phone definitely stopped the sales process.

Picture a different conversation with another service provider:

Agent: "Mr. Pearlal is your cell phone service currently on contract or prepaid."

Me: "it's on contract."

Agent: "Are you currently enjoying the benefits of being on a contract package?"

Me: "Yes."

Agent: "Mr. Pearlal, my company has recently introduced a contract package that I think you would also truly enjoy. Before I can tell you all about it, I would like to ask you a couple of questions."

See how the above conversation moves the sales process forward; before I knew it, I was sharing information about my current mobile phone contract package.

That, by the way, did move the sales process forward.

The better way to get attention

Getting your prospect's attention shouldn't be rocket

science and does not require some cheesy statement to keep your prospect on the phone.

Many sales people think that statements like "What if I would save you some money on your car insurance?" will get a client to respond in kind.

The truth is, using statements like these, you set yourself up for a hard sell; which is not the desired result.

If you are not able to save the prospect money, then you have no sale and no way of bouncing back to a state where you can change your position.

With the many years in the call center, I found the simplest and easiest way to get attention is to call your prospect by his name. "Good morning, Joe?" or "Good morning, Mr. Williams?"

As a child when your parents called your name, you responded. To move the sales process forward, say something that will elicit a response from your prospect. "Good morning, Mr. Prospect," does just that.

As mentioned before, in general, people will respond in kind. Your prospect will respond positively to a positive call.

By the same note, a negative call will get a negative response. Keep in mind that if the client hangs up on you, that too is a response and you need to evaluate why your prospects responded in that 'Kind'. I will elaborate a little bit more on this in handling responses and objections.

Be polite and kind, and you will be responded to in politeness and kindness. Try to be witty and smart and that is exactly the response you should expect.

2. Gather Information

The first part of the sales process should never take your more than 120 seconds to complete. Two minutes is more than enough to 'Get attention' - in the process, you need to identify yourself and give a reason for your call.

The second part of the sales process is the key to your entire SELLING process – information and presentation. Gathering information should be a conversation between yourself and your client, more specifically it should be a structured conversation.

What information do you need to be gathering?

Good question! If you are selling a product or service that will get your clients to do what they do better than they are doing currently, you need to gather as much information about how they can achieve that.

If your product gives your clients 'peace of mind' as in the case of insurance, then gather information about what bothers and worries your clients; i.e. knowing they will not be left stranded without a car in case they are in an accident.

If your product is designed to give your prospects increased pleasure, then find out what information you will need to give them just that. Asking questions is the best way to know how I can help my clients.

The most basic questions I ask fall into the following categories:

NEED: *Do you currently have what I have to offer. If YES, how long have you had it and how much are you paying?*

NEED: *Are you looking to replace or to add? Replacing what or adding by how much?*

These questions determine whether my prospective client is a new buyer or an existing buyer. And if they are looking to replace or add. I want to know if I am competing or complementing.

CLIENT VALUES: *Who or what is this product for? Is this for themselves or for someone else? E.g. Is the life cover for a Home Loan or are you doing the responsible thing by providing for your family? Whatever the response, probe further about what they value.*

CLIENT VALUES: *Why is it important that they have what I have to offer? E.g. does the bank require a Life Insurance before they can give you the home loan? Will the dealership not release the car without confirmation of Car Insurance etc?*

These questions help me to understand what is valuable to my client. REMEMBER! Clients want something of value. With that, my selling approach would focus on whatever is valuable – saving money, their child's dreams, their car, their happiness, etc.

COMMITMENT: *When do you want to start or take delivery of what I have to offer? Is it immediately, or immediate future? E.g. when do you want to start your cover, immediately or month end? On what day do you want it to start?*

Always get a commitment. Without a commitment, your sales process is based on HOPE without the EXPECTATION that your client will BUY.

Gather as much information as possible to help your

client make an informed buying decision. When you have all the information you need to make your presentation, increase passion, stand up, gather enthusiasm and make the best presentation.

Finally, close like a superstar.

3. *Make your presentation*

Your presentation should NOT be boring and mundane. With every word, paint a picture for your client to give them the best idea of what you have to offer.

I always get asked the question *"How do I do an interesting and captivating presentation?"*

How do you create the imagery of a product or service your client can barely see, touch or feel; at least not at the time of doing your presentation?

Here's how:

Posture

Voice projection is everything in your presentation. You want your client to hear you clearly without sounding like you are shouting. The only way your voice will be bold with confidence is if you're standing or sitting up straight.

Many sales agents make sales on the floor while seated, the truth is, it is possible, but you will close better when you're on your feet and upright.

Tonality

It's not always what you say that gets your prospect interested in what you have to offer but also how you say it. If you tell your client "this is the best offer" you better sound and feel like you're offering the best.

Working in a call center can sometimes be tiring because you're tired of doing the same thing over and over again.

If you want to succeed in making SUPERSTAR SALES, you'll need to keep your energy up. If something is meant to sound sad, say it with sadness. If it is meant to ignite excitement, say it with excitement.

Remember your voice is your face, how you say what you say will make all the difference. Begin a call with a smile. From time to time where appropriate, laugh. It only adds flavor to your tonality.

Pace

With human beings becoming more and more dependent on their technological devices to store and retrieve information, recent studies show our concentration span has become worse than that of a goldfish – less than 9 seconds to be exact.

I don't know how true this is, but if that's the case, you better pace yourself. The idea is to move fast enough for your client to absorb your offer yet not too slow to bore your client to death.

K.I.S.S (Keep it simple, stupid.)

Your presentation should be simple enough that intellectually challenged prospects will understand what you're selling, but also professional enough not to insult the intellect of those well-informed clients.

Keep it simple, keep it basic and if there is any additional information your client needs to know, let the client ask. Remember your presentation is personalized based on information gathered from your client. While many clients may share similarities, every one of your prospective clients is a unique individual that needs to be attended to with care.

4. *Close your sale*

Applying the Winning Formula. It's all good and well to know the success formula, however without ever applying what you have learnt is no different to you having a map to the desired destination but never really starting your journey.

Imagine if on a movie set the director shouted, 'lights, camera...' but never action; no movie would ever reach the big screens or the small screens for that matter. Knowledge is good, the application of such knowledge is better.

Knowledgeable application is the greatest.

The only thing standing between you and the successful implementation of the SALES SUPERSTAR WINNING FORMULA is a simple number – 72:21. Seventy-two, twenty-one? you ask? Yes 72:21. It represents 72 hours 21 days.

If you are the kind of person who likes to learn more about the work they do so they can get better at doing what they do, this will not be the first time you are applying your mind to learning something new and useful to advance your career.

If you learn something today with the hope of applying it, chances are, if you do not act on your new found knowledge within 72 hours, you will find yourself 6 months down the line with little or no result of what you have learned.

The second principle to the number 72:21 basically says, because SUCCESS IS THE HABIT of doing whatever produces the desired results, and habits are born out of repetition. In order for your new found knowledge to form part of your habits of success, you'll need to practice and action them for a series of 21 days.

After which they form a habit and become a part of who you are. So you can read this book all you want, but if you do not take action within 72 hours consistently and repetitively over a period of 21 days, you will not succeed.

The mind is designed to retract to a comfort zone, a place where nothing is new and everything remains the same.

The mind is happy with normal and ordinary and avoids abnormal and extraordinary. Success is not for normal or ordinary people, because, let's face it; to be successful in sales you'll have to do the abnormal and the extraordinary.

You'll have to be willing to go against the grain and do what most people won't in order to have what most people don't. Whatever you learn from this book, start soon; you have 72 hours and 21 days to change your life. Implement what you can while you get into the habit of learning something NEW.

Begin With the End in Mind

I find it very fascinating that many SALES PEOPLE in the call center are driven by HOPE. Not that there is anything wrong with hope, but I need you to know expectation is better than hope.

When a farmer goes out into the fields to plow, he does so EXPECTING his crop to grow and bear fruit.

The same applies to sales in the call center; begin every call expecting a sale. Not because you HOPE to convince your client that your product or service is what they are looking for but because you value your contribution to your prospect's needs.

Begin your call with the EXPECTATION that it is a sale and a lot more calls will turn into sales than hopeful conversations.

It is not just the SALE you should be expecting. You should also be EXPECTING your prospect to be responding, objecting and questioning what you have to offer.

A good lawyer friend of mine always says, "Never make a statement or ask a question to which you cannot expect or anticipate the response." It is in this spirit that I say, expect and anticipate the responses, objections and the questions that may be posed by your prospect.

If a response is new to you, learn it and practice how you will handle it the next time you are faced with it.

All Roads Lead To Rome

Remember how I said the purpose of every step in the sales process has one objective, and one objective only – to move the sales process forward.

The only reason you are calling or taking your call is to have your prospect's attention. The only reason you want to keep your prospects attention is because you want to gather information.

The only reason you are gathering information is to do a presentation and the purpose of your presentation is to close the sale. At all times be truthful with your prospect as you walk them through the buying experience. REMEMBER, people hate to be sold to but they love to buy. Help them buy what you have to offer.

The Recipe for Success

If the formula is what you do to be successful, the recipe is how you do it. Many cooks have the formula, but very few cooks get the recipe right to the T.

If the call center business wanted robotic delivery of their sales process, they can easily do this, especially given the advancement in technology. Getting the delivery right, you need to put forward the following elements, your skills, and your knowledge, but most of all, your PERSONALITY.

PERSONALITY is what brings the FORMULA to life. It makes scripting sound natural and easy to accept and understand.

PERSONALITY is the style by which you grab your prospect's attention, gather information, make your presentation and close your sale.

The best part about any movie showcase is that every director that does a great piece of work soon enough gets noticed for their style. I cannot teach style or PERSONALITY.

Only you will know what flavor you bring to THE FORMULA. All I can do is encourage you to bring your sales process to life with a little bit more PERSONALITY.

Follow Up and Follow Through

The expectation is, every call SHOULD be a sale. But as you know, it happens that your client does NOT buy immediately. From time to time you will have to do what many call center salespeople dread the most – follow up. I'm not very fond of the word follow up, it creates the idea that you are chasing after your prospect to buy something they do not already need or want.

I like the word FOLLOW THROUGH because it simply means finishing what you started. A lot of CALL CENTER SALES people take the position that a follow through with a prospect is like recovering from a rejection, and that is not true.

Follow through is giving your prospect a second opportunity to say 'YES'. To illustrate this, let me share with you some scripting that is very common with the average call center sale person.

Agent: "Good morning Joe. It's Steven here calling you from ABC Insurance Company. I was calling to find out how you would like to proceed with our discussion."

Prospect: "Mmm. Ahhh. I think I will pass on this one."

Every time a prospect asks you to call later because they have not made the decision; without sounding pushy, ask your prospect what it is they are not certain about that you can clarify.

At least you will know why they are not making the decision at that moment and are able to handle the response in order to MOVE THE SALES PROCESS FORWARD.

Always handle responses and objection, and CLOSE.

Handle the response by offering your product "…are you HAPPY with what I have to offer?"

Find out what they need to think about. If they are not happy, offer what they will be happy with. If it is about price, offer more value for the same price or offer what they can afford to start with.

Get the commitment on when they want to start and close.

Remember, every call can be a sale if you able to KNOW YOUR CLIENTS NEEDS AND WANTS, KNOW YOUR CLIENTS VALUES, AND GET COMMITMENT.

***

"When obstacles arise, you change your direction to reach your goal; you do not change your decision to get there."

- Zig Ziglar

SALES SUPERSTAR

Chapter 8

HANDLING RESPONSES AND OBJECTIONS

SALES SUPERSTARS are not people you would consider to be normal. Normal is not a word we're familiar with, nor is the word ordinary.

With RESPONSES AND OBJECTIONS, most sales people are hoping they never happen, I truly look forward to them.

I know my sales process needs to be short, sweet and straight to the point.

The only reason I look forward to responses or objections is one reason alone – it allows me to do the following:

1. Sell myself

2. Sell my company

3. Sell my benefits

Still don't get it? Read on, I will explain.

Before we go there, let's first deal with the most common responses and objections at hand.

Most Common Response

Despite that we expect a sale from every call, not every prospect we speak to will say 'YES' or at least without some kind of resistance.

Contrary to popular belief, objections are not an invitation to battle out the merits of a sale. An objection is a response to how the client views the value of your product, their need for the product as well as timeliness and affordability of your product.

Of all the responses or objections I get from the people I speak to, I find that no matter what they say, their responses fall into one of five categories:

NEED: Thank you, but I am not interested

NEED: I'm happy with what I've got

TIMELINESS: I'm too busy to talk right now

AUTHORITY: Let me speak to ....

VALUE: Send me something to read

VALUE: Budget doesn't allow or the price is too high.

To even consider yourself a SALES SUPERSTAR, or at least a Sales Superstar in the making, you need to learn to EXPECT, ANTICIPATE AND HANDLE any of the above responses or objections.

Thank you, but I am not interested

Not a day goes by where I don't get the response, "Thank you, but I am not interested."

You'd expect this to happen a lot in the outbound skill set because you are calling out; but having worked in an inbound skill set for more than 5 years, I have come to realize the experience is just the same.

Now, imagine receiving a message from a prospect that clearly showed interest by requesting to be called and they still tell you:

"Thank you, but I am not Interested."

If you thought you were alone, think again; it is a common thread with every call center.

I'm sure you would agree with me, there have been many moments where the prospect initially said they were 'not interested' but ended up buying your product anyway.

The true essence of SUPERSTAR sales is selling to someone that is not initially interested in what you have to offer until they learn the value of what you have to offer.

My response to 'Thank you, but I'm not interested.' is so simple it will scare you.

Prospect: "No thank you, but I am not interested."

Me: "Well, Mr. Jones, a lot of my clients started off not being interested until they experienced what we had to offer."

You notice there are two things that happened there.

Firstly I made the client feel okay about 'not being interested'; with reference to my other clients, I already gave him ownership of the client-provider relationship.

Secondly, I created the image that this is not just a product but an experience. I was honest with my prospect. 'Yes,' many of my clients started off without interest. I gave my prospect a reason to belong to an experience many others before him have had and would not want to leave him out. But most of all, the sales process moves forward to the next step.

No thanks, I'm happy with what I've got

If I asked you how many shoes you have, I am sure it will be more than one pair. Why do you need more than one pair when you have only one set of feet. You have your reasons, but the fact remains, you have more than one pair.

The second part to think about with this response is, some people are genuinely happy with what they have.

It's called the status quo or the comfort zone and change is not something humans want to go through, even though change is the only constant.

As a CALL CENTER AGENT, you will get your once-in-a-while client calling in because they are not happy with what they have and want to replace, this is not about them.

This is about those that will not call and your job is to convince them you're either the better option to what they need or a great complement to what they have.

In the life insurance industry, I can tell you this, your clients either have existing life insurance, not enough or none at all. Your role is to fill the gap between any of the three options.

Your main objective is to move the sales process onto the second level where you gather information, "No thanks, I'm happy with what I've got" should not be a barrier in any way.

I'm too busy to talk right now

Let's face it, life can get hectic sometimes. One of the most frequently asked questions to people training call center sales agents is "When is the best time to call".

The answer to that question is simple, anytime, all the time. There used to be a time when the world was only as far as the eye could see, before the birth of airplanes and internet connectivity. When the sun was down, people were either having dinner or sleeping. Times have changed; people work and operate 24 hours a day, 7 days a week.

This is not to say you need to be calling 24 hours a day and 7 days a week; it only means whenever you call, there is always someone ready to hear you out. When your prospect utters the words, "I'm too busy to talk right now", rest assured, there is someone ready to hear you out. I normally respond with "What time is better for you to talk?"

I have read many sales books and sales gurus teach that you should try to convince your prospect to speak to you right then; with tactics such as "All I need is 5 minutes of your time" or "This will not take too much of your time, I will be very short and brief".

The trouble with such tactics is you're literally digging a hole for yourself because you set up an expectation about how long the process might be, and if the process becomes a second longer than you promised; you have been dishonest and the client has no reason to trust anything you say from then on.

When I say people respond in kind. If you show respect for their time, they will do the same for you.

I know one or two sales agents will in protest say, "But clients lie all the time." They tell you they are busy, please call them later, and when you call later, they do not pick up the phone.

There is an upside and a downside to this. I always think I would rather spend my time speaking to someone who wants to listen than waste my time chasing after someone who does not show the same respect I show towards them. It's that simple.

Remember, most of your prospects actually want your offer, some would like to have whatever you have to offer, and others would just not be bothered.

Deal with those that want to hear you out, don't waste your time on those that DON'T.

Send me something to read

Have you ever received marketing material from a company trying to sell you something you thought you might need but never really featured as a priority on your list of activities? Did you ever read the material? Maybe 'Yes'; but most definitely 'No'.

There are two basic reasons why any prospect or client would ask you to send something to read; you either said too much, they are confused about what they are buying or they are too ashamed to tell you their real reason so they hide behind *"send me something to read"*

Honesty is my policy, since objections and responses are reactions that should be anticipated and expected, ask your client the simple question, *"is there something I have not made clear about what we have to offer?"*

With life insurance, after I give premium and ask "Are you HAPPY with that?" some clients will ask me to send a quote or something to read so they can think about it. I anticipate such responses and reactions, and the best way to respond to such a response is by repeating your product;

'Are you happy with the cover and the premium?'

Basically, you want to know if the client is HAPPY with what you have to offer. Normally this is when the real reason will show up, where they either say they are NOT HAPPY and they tell you what they are NOT HAPPY with.

REMEMBER! The purpose or objective of every step of the sales process is to move the sales process forward.

If the client is NOT HAPPY with your offer, ask what would make them HAPPY and offer that.

If it is price, ask the client what price they would COMMIT to. Get confirmation by saying "If I can get you the PRICE you are happy with, would you start on the agreed date." Making the client accountable to their commitment.

Allow me to illustrate with an example:

Me: You have a MILLION in life cover, HALF A MILLION in disability cover, and a cash back bonus after 5years. All this and more value than any other insurer would offer. Your premium is only 1000. ARE YOU HAPPY WITH THAT?

Client: Please send me the quote and I will come back to you.

Me: I get that you would like me to send you a quote, but ARE YOU HAPPY WITH THE COVER AND THE PREMIUM.

Client: The premium is a lot higher that I was expecting.

Me: What were you expecting, sir?

Client: Between 500 and 600

Me: If I can get your premium to between 500 and 600 will you then start your cover at the beginning of next month.

Client: Yes

Then you work your magic to get the premium to between 500 and 600. You can lower the cover, move a benefit or do whatever you must do to get your client what they want.

This applies to the value of what they want, the price or anything the client is NOT HAPPY with.

It's not within my budget

Most people would love to drive the most expensive car, but because they cannot afford it; they don't. Sounds simple? Not really. Price is relative. Think about yourself, when you last went shopping at the mall with the aim of buying yourself a 48 inch TV screen which you have been wanting for a long time. Let's say you get to the shop and you find the sale is over and the price is no longer 75% off. You are forced to pay the full price. When you did have the money, did you turn back and wait another day or did you go out of your budget to get what you wanted.

Being of Indian decent, I am always looking for a bargain. It's sometimes so bad even when the item is on discount, I try to negotiate a discount on the discounted price. It's human nature to look for the best value at the best price.

With pricing, as a SALES SUPERSTAR, your job is to increase the VALUE of whatever you are selling and therefore making the price the client has to pay very insignificant.

What You Need To Be Selling

When your clients buy your product or service, in essence, there are three things they are buying, that is you, the company you represent and the benefits your products and services will offer to reduce pain or increase pleasure and satisfaction or solve a problem they have.

When you do your presentation, handling objections or responding to reactions and questions, remember what you are selling, yourself, the company and the benefits.

Selling yourself

People buy from people they like and admire.

The SALES SUPERSTAR approach makes your client want to buy from you and no one else. This has everything to do with how you sell yourself through service - what you say and what you do.

Go as far as offering your direct line of contact or your email address. Tell them how you will bend over backward to give them value for money.

After all, this is your client in the making. Make a promise and keep it.

Selling your company

People support brands and companies they know will take care of them and live up to their promise.

It should be noted that not every company has won the award for best service, most claims paid out, least rejected claims or the most cost effective.

There is always something good about your company.

If there is nothing good you can say about your company, maybe you shouldn't be working there in the first place.

So sell your company.

Tell your prospective client about the service awards your company has won. Tell your client about the positive feedback and reviews you received from other clients.

When it comes from your lips, it's not boasting, it's simply highlighting the reason why your client should buy from you and not your competitor.

Selling your benefits

Remember what I said earlier about selling and telling. Do get confused with the two. There's a very good reason why I say SELL YOUR BENEFITS and not tell your client about the benefits.

If the benefit to your solution is the saving money, SELL the benefit of saving by highlighting the many other things your clients would do with the money they save. If the benefit is about convenience and comfort for your client, SELL that in such a way your client sees value in what you have to offer.

Whatever the benefit is to your client, don't just tell them about it. SELL IT.

First Call Resolution Closing

Your environment may be different and with a friend or two that come from a face-to-face sales background, I can confidently say the best sale in the Call Center is the sale closed on the first day.

Whatever can be said about building relationships, following up and following through. Strive to get your sale on the first call. A good friend of mine, who was also a Manager in the department I work in made famous the acronym FDC; which simply meant FIRST DAY CLOSING.

People who have bothered to research and study the sales cycle, especially the call center sales cycle, know that you only have one shot to MAKE OR BREAK the sale. The longer it takes to get your client's commitment, the less likely it is they will commit.

Try to remember a time when you saw a movie and you were so convinced it was the greatest movie ever made. Bruce Lee always did it for me. He made martial arts look like child's play. As I grew older, I still loved Bruce Lee, but my admiration and adoration diminished over time.

In call center sales, a day of indecision by your client is a lifetime into the possibility of never getting a decision. I have learned, to be frank with my clients.

I remember once a client called in looking for a "QUOTE" for life cover. The first thing I said was, "I understand you need a quote, I will go one step further and give you the cover you need."

This might sound cocky to the average advisor, but I was definitely within my powers to tell the client that; while everything begins with a "quote", the cover was what he was looking for and I was the person to give it to him.

Needless to say, when I came to the closing, I simply wanted to know if my client was "Happy with what I had to offer!" and when he said yes, I asked for banking details and closed like a SUPERSTAR.

Selling is not hard if you know HOW.

Every SUPERSTAR has something to offer the world. The world of Call Center sales needs a SUPER HERO like you.

***

"Every 'NO' is
a step closer to
a 'YES'."

- Mark Cuban

Chapter 9

SALES TIPS AND TACTICS

Every Call Center sale person I know could do with a sales tip or tactic to get you that one more sale.

This book has more than enough to learn from but I know a SELLING tip can always come in handy when you need it.

The following list may not be the complete list of all sales tips and tactics that form the foundation of the SALES SUPERSTAR WINNING FORMULA, but they are a good start.

Use them well; and as you grow and become better at what you do, I'm sure there are some tips or tactics that work for you that might also work for another advisor, write them down and share them.

I share these with the expectation they'll get you closing more sales each day.

1
Quickly Build Rapport

The best call center sales people not only sell but also sell a relationship with themselves and the company they represent.

Three things need to stand out in order to quickly build trust and establish an excellent relationship with the customer:

1. **Be Confident** – Confidence quickly builds rapport with your client because it gives them the comfort of knowing they're dealing with someone who knows what they are doing.

2. **Be Natural** – No one says you cannot use a script. But also no actor's ever succeeded sounding like they were reading from a script. Keep it natural; learn your script before. Internalize it with your personality. Let the script be you not the other way around

3. **Listen More** – Something that should come naturally to anyone working in the call center; you have two ears and one mouth for a reason, to listen twice as much as you talk. True listening involves things like 'verbal nods' like 'uh-huh', and 'I see', paraphrasing back what someone has just said to you and asking further questions about a piece of information the customer has just given you.

2
Take Control, Keep Control

No one knows the sales process better than you.

You're the expert at what you do. How you lead from the beginning of the call will determine the direction of the call. You will either sell or be sold to.

Remember these three principles when you navigate your client through the sales process.

1. **Call your client by name** – This is very crucial, a lot of the time, when you call your client by name, they will treat you as an equal or better yet, as their trusted advisor.

2. **Explain the process** – A great leader knows to let his or her followers know where they are going before they start the journey. Always give your client a brief explanation of the process by which you will get them to be a satisfied customer.

3. **Be frank and honest** – Nothing will make you lose control of your sales process faster than sugar coating the realities of your client's situation. Let your 'NO' be a 'NO' and your 'YES' be a 'YES'. Even when the client attempts to sugar coat their situation, be real and be honest.

3
Get Early Buy-In

People hate to be sold to, but they love to buy. The best thing you can do for your client is making them aware of the decision they'll have to make at the end of the call – and that decision requires commitment.

Let your client COMMIT to a solution that will work for them.

1. **Early Commitment** – Remember what I said about your PRODUCT? Early in the conversation always ask your client, "If you're HAPPY with what I have to offer you, when do you want to get started?"

2. **Give Options** – This could easily fall into taking control and keeping control. But for the sake of simplicity let this be about getting early BUY IN from your client. "If you are HAPPY, when do you want to get started? End of this month or the next month?" Either, Or? Option 1 or Option 2? Always give closed ended options.

3. **Assume The Sale** - Always expect that if the client is ready and willing to go through the SELLING process, they are ready and willing to BUY. Remember, SELLING is a logical process, BUYING is an emotional experience.

4
Mind your Language

Your words and tone are to the call center what body language is to face-to-face sales. The words you use say a lot about you and your thoughts. Minding your language does not mean you have to speak very formal when it's not necessary. Minding your language means be aware of the words you use.

1. **Use Positive Words** – Using positive words will re-affirm the response you expect from the client. After your needs analysis statement say something like "...I am sure YOU WOULD AGREE WITH ME that your family would need the financial support when you are no longer there to provide for them." It is rare that a client would disagree with you.

2. **Confirm With Reassurance** – Whenever a client makes a choice on options you give, always confirm the choice with reassurance. "Is it going to be option 1 or options 2?" Client says "Option 2." You say with reassurance "That is an excellent choice."

3. **Tend to Numbers** – When it comes to price, reduce it by adding words like "It is ONLY 500." "It will be an INVESTMENT OF ONLY 200" When it comes to value, pump up the number "Half a million sounds better than five hundred thousand."

5
Don't Take No for an Answer

This might sound like something out of a HARD SELLING sales book. It isn't. The Sales Superstar way of thinking says "Where there's a need, there's a SALE." Everything else – PRICE, TIMING, AUTHORITY etc. is all negotiable.

1. **ABC (Always Be Closing)** – Handle every objection with simplicity and close. The only time you should be handling objections is when you close, anything in between is nothing more than a response from your client. For this reason, always positively handle an objection and close.

2. **KISS (Keep It Simple Stupid)** – Too much information may lead to confusion. Keep it simple. Give ONLY what is necessary to make a decision.

3. **STF (Start To Finish)** – I have to admit, this one I just made up, but it is just as important and just as powerful. Your client's greatest fear is CHANGE and DISAPPOINTMENT. Keep talking to your client until they see the VALUE of your product. Remember ABC, after every objection or response and no matter how many 'NOs' you get, close just one more time. Finish what you START.

6

Be Solution Focused

It's not just about the sale. Remember, you are providing a viable solution to the needs and wants of your client. Focus on the solution. A well crafted solution to a need will always result in a sale.

1. **Persistence and patience -** These go hand in hand. While the objection is to get your client to agree with what you have to offer, never let your emotions take control of the main objective of providing a viable solution for your client.

2. **Accountability –** This goes both ways, to you as the advisor and the clients you are assisting. Hold yourself accountable to your goals, achieving what you set out to achieve; assisting the client and providing a viable solution. Also, hold your client accountable to their objective of finding a solution to their problem, when they make a commitment, hold them to it.

3. **Insight –** Your client might not always know they have a need or a problem that need to be solved. As the expert in your field it is your responsibility to make them aware of the benefits of the solution you provide. Don't be afraid to remind the client, you are an expert in your field.

7

Grow Some Balls

I can't think of any other way to say this. As a sales superstar in the Call Center, guts is what will separate you from the average Call Center sales agent.

After all, you're not just a call center agent, you're a sales superstar.

1. **Don't be afraid to ask the hard questions.** The focus on trying to offend the clients is the reason why many Call Center agents are afraid to ask the hard questions.

   Questions like, "when do you want to start?"or "If you are not happy with the price, does is make sense that I still send you a quote?"

   It also helps to explain why you ask the questions you are. E.g. "I am asking because I want to know how I can assist you further"

2. **It's not what you say but how you say it.** Don't confuse confidence with cockiness. When reasoning with a client, remember how you say it matters just as much as what you're saying.

   Avoid sounding like you are arguing. Use a reasoning tone. With the right tonality, the right words, at the right pitch; you become a trusted advisor not a bulldozing sales person.

3. **Selling is logical, buying is emotional.** Research shows that people buy more with their emotion than logic.

Tap into the emotional connection of why they need your product or service.

If it is fear or doubt, expose the fear, increase their doubt. After-all they're better off with your product or service than without.

Get rich or dial trying.

– Yogesh Pearlal

About the Author

Yogesh Pearlal is the #1 Call Center Sales Advisor at one of South Africa's leading Insurance companies. With a career that spans more than 12 years, Yogesh Pearlal has consistently been the #1 Sales Advisor on the phone for more than 8 years running.

In his first book Sales Superstar – The Winning Formula to Call Center Sales; He maintains there is a formula to consistent sales success especially in an industry when consistency is not a guarantee. His consistent performance has won him many awards from 3 Months to 6 Months Incentive Bonuses and a couple of holiday travels.

Born and raised in Durban's notorious Chatsworth, now dubbed to be the hottest commodity in the Call Center industry, Yogesh Pearlal has managed to achieve a great amount of success all while working in the Call Center.

If you've ever
picked up a phone
to convince a total
stranger to BUY
whatever you were
SELLING, but for
some reason have not
succeeded,
THIS BOOK IS FOR
YOU.

All the Best.
And God Bless.

redOystor

AN INVITATION FROM THE PUBLISHER

Join us at www.redoystor.com or connect with us on facebook and twitter @redOystor to be part of a community of people who love the very best in books and reading.

Whether you want to discover more about the author or the book, read more about upcoming events, interviews or watch trailers, or have a chance to win early limited editions, we think you will like what you are looking for.

And if you don't, let us know what's missing through our contact us page or email us at **theEditor@redoystor.com**

We love what we do, and we'd love you to be a part of it.

www.redoystor.com

www.ingramcontent.com/pod-product-compliance
Lightning Source LLC
Chambersburg PA
CBHW022040190326
41520CB00008B/659